CW01084124

The Power of Your Heart

Loving the Self

Gabriella Kortsch, Ph.D.

Praise for *Rewiring the Soul*

"*Rewiring the Soul* is a revelation of insight into the foundations of human suffering and transcendence. It not only lays out the essential steps for inner freedom and joy but it also illuminates the way to true human potential: the stunning and dynamic "Possible Self." Written with clarity, compassion and wisdom, this chronicle is not one of mere speculation, but arises from the depths of hard won personal experience. Gabriella Kortsch is a spiritual master for our time."
Paul Rademacher, Executive Director, The Monroe Institute; author of *A Spiritual Hitchhiker's Guide to the Universe*

"Gabriella Kortsch uses her talent and experience to write the instruction manual on rewiring the soul. An in-depth guide on life, love, spiritual evolution and our integration within the universe."
Michael Habernig & April Hannah; Producers of *The Path: The Afterlife* and The Path 11 Documentaries

"This meticulously researched and crafted book is clearly the masterwork of a profoundly gifted healer of the soul, one who thinks deeply, feels deeply, and cares deeply about the well-being of the world and its humankind. Reading it will change your life; beginning to live actively any of its ideas, principles, and suggestions will *transform* your life. And bring you safely and joyfully home to your true self, your soul. I found it dazzling, challenging, and wondrously useful."
Peggy Rubin, Director, Center for Sacred Theatre, Ashland, Oregon; author of *To Be and How To Be, Transforming Your Life Through Sacred Theatre*

"*Rewiring the Soul* is a thoughtful guide to the peace and joy that self-government through inner awareness brings. In the words of author Gabriella Kortsch, anyone's ideal 'possible human' becomes their actual reality by following the simple inner steps in this remarkable book."
Jim Wawro; author of *Ask Your Inner Voice*

"*Rewiring the Soul* is the human being's directory to the soul. This inspirational book asks you to simply open yourself to the possibility that you are much more than you have considered yourself to be; in truth, you are spirit in form living a soul-directed life. It is a breakthrough for those seeking practical assistance, those of a more mystical bent, and every soul awaiting discovery. Read it cover to cover first; then place it close at hand to pick up every time your mind strays from your soul's message radiating from within the heart."
Toni Petrinovich, Ph.D.; author of *The Call: Awakening the Angelic Human*

"I thought I could pick just one chapter to write a review, but I couldn't …. I was glued to the chair as I read *Rewiring the Soul* … a literary, in-depth masterpiece to the human psyche, behavior and ultimate transformation. Exquisitely written, beautifully executed."
Ali Rodriguez, Business Coach, co-author of *Mastering the Art of Success* with Jack Canfield and Mark Victor Hansen

"*Rewiring the Soul* is one the best introductions to the spiritual life I've ever read. Not esoteric but real-world and practical. Read it and Soul is no longer just a dogma, nor hypothesis, it is made real and as much a part of your being as your toes. We usually shut off our inner voice, yet by recognizing this aspect of ourselves we begin to discover our essential nature, our intuitive truth, and that becomes our loving guide. The author illustrates the limitations of living only as the mind's Ego, and demonstrates in practical terms how we can transcend this by awakening a conscious viewpoint, following the path of our intuition and feelings, no longer separated from our body and the reality around us, and integrating at last our Soul's inner guidance and wellspring of love. The implications are profound."
Peter Shepherd; Founder, TransForMind; author of *Daring To Be Yourself*

"A glance at the contents of *Rewiring the Soul* will tell you much about the values promoted: *awareness, freedom, peace and love.* I fully agree with the author that it is all about re-connecting with our authentic 'loving self': it is only then that we can deeply

transform our life while also inspiring a transformation in the lives of others! Through this powerful book, Gabriella Kortsch *honestly* shares her love of serving the inner potential and the spiritual growth of human beings with passion, joy and commitment."
Elisabetta Franzoso; International Speaker, Coach, author of ***Stella's Mum Gets Her Groove Back: A True Story***

"The Soul doesn't get sick but it does need nourishment; if not it seems as if our life starves to death. This wonderful book by Dr. Gabriella Kortsch is definitely healthy "Soul food". It becomes clear that as the personality endeavors to "rewire" the Soul, it is its own energy or conscious awareness that is elevated to that higher level where the invisible becomes visible and experienced as peace, joy, love and freedom. A treat to enjoy and celebrate."
Eric Rolf; author of ***Soul Medicine: The Heart of Healing***

"This book is a gift to humanity, a valuable tool in aiding seekers to accomplish mastery of their own lives. Gabriella Kortsch provides clear steps to help people find peace in a practical and powerful way. She does not ask you to give up anything other than what no longer serves you. Brilliantly written!"
Hillary Raimo; Author & Radio Host

Praise for *The Tao of Spiritual Partnership*

"All humans seek the illusive touch of another's Soul, which opens us to the sense of belonging to something bigger than the self. Dr. Kortsch has given us the true "tao" of relationship in this brilliant exploration of emotional tapestry. Through her wise teaching, we can not only discover ourselves in the reflection of our partners, but we can learn how to access a *spiritual* connection that sets us free. We will be grateful for this illumination of spiritual partnership for generations to come. Thank You, Gabriella."
Chris Griscom: Spiritual Leader, Author of *Ecstasy is a New Frequency* & *Time Is an Illusion*

"In my years of researching life plans and soul contracts, I've learned that we plan (before we're born) to have romantic relationships for the purposes of healing and expansion. And this is just what Gabriella Kortsch so eloquently and comprehensively shows you in The Tao of Spiritual Partnership: how your primary love relationship may be a sacred vessel that transports you and your partner to a place of mutual healing and expansion."
Robert Schwartz: Author of *Your Soul's Gift: The Healing Power of the Life You Planned Before You Were Born*

"Gabriella Kortsch has a rich international background with unmatched experience in her field. *The Tao of Spiritual Partnership* is a unique blend of wit and wisdom; she encourages us to take responsibility for our relationships, while recognizing and seizing the opportunities for our own personal spiritual growth."
William Buhlman, Author of *Adventures Beyond the Body*

"*The Tao of Spiritual Partnership* is an excellent, smart guide to making your relationships blossom. Your partner will thank you for buying this book! Why struggle with relationships when you can have a fulfilling spiritual partnership? Dr. Gabriella Kortsch's newest book *The Tao of Spiritual Partnership* deftly shows the way to satisfying interactions with the loves of your life."
Jim Wawro, Author of *Awakening Counsel: A Practical Guide to Creating the Life You Want to Live.*

"Riveting introduction into the author's life, authentically reflecting her years of personal development and truths. I cried, I reflected, and then I merged my soul with the truthfulness of the facts as presented. Gabriella Kortsch takes us through a journey that covers most aspects of human relationships from new-born to adult, leading us into the power and path of Spiritual Partnerships and what it all means, what to do with it, and how to apply it to our lives, in this precise moment in time. The importance of fulfillment of a life well-lived through understanding and practicing self-love is paramount and candidly expressed in this one-of-a-kind book. I have gained deeper insights into my own life, and the promise of the book: "to love without needing" is profoundly delivered!"
Ali R. Rodriguez: Business Coach Strategist, Co-Author of *Mastering the Art of Success*

Praise for *The Power of Your Heart: Loving the Self*

"In *The Power of Your Heart*, Dr. Kortsch takes the well known self-help axiom of "first, one must love oneself, before one can love others" and proceeds to deliver nothing less than a profound and authentic way of living and being that heals the soul and improves one's interactions and relationships with others. By clearly distinguishing her love-based concept of self-love from the fear-based concepts of narcissism, egotism, and neediness, Dr. Kortsch provides a step by step guide that, if honestly applied, puts one on a life's path of peace, satisfaction, contentment, and happiness."
Thomas Campbell; author of *My Big TOE*

"From childhood we are taught to mercilessly nitpick our essential being in pursuit of a mythical perfection. With deep insight and impeccable clarity, Dr. Gabriella Kortsch, Ph.D., turns the tables to illuminate the liberation possible when loving ourselves unconditionally. In so doing, she provides a road map to undiscovered bliss and wholeness. A must-read for anyone on the path to self-understanding!"
Paul Rademacher, Author of *A Spiritual Hitchhiker's Guide to the Universe: Travel Tips for the Spiritually Perplexed,* CEO of Lucid Greening, Editor of *Inner Story Magazine*

"This book explains the vital importance of loving yourself and why that is not in the least bit selfish. If there is a lot of love inside you, then you have more to share, in fact, it becomes a bottomless well. With love in your heart, your choices will be based on understanding, compassion and empathy. An inspiring read!"
Peter Shepherd; Founder, TransForMind; author of *Daring To Be Yourself*

"*The Power of Your Heart* is a book to satisfy the soul's hunger and deserves to be read by every adult, parent, teacher and adolescent. It assures us that it is not just permissible, but essential, to love ourselves, undoing the conditioning that has kept us in a state of

unworthiness and self-doubt, and sets us on the path to emotional, psychological, and spiritual growth. Love of self is a prerequisite to love of others and love is the foundation on which we are building a new world of compassion, joy and good will."
Linda Stitt; Author of *Acting My Age*

In the art of loving the self, this book takes the phrase 'self help' to the next level. Gabriella Kortsch has made the case and built the foundation that ultimately will become your own self-empowering path to true happiness and prosperity. Using real world situations along with quotes from the masters scattered throughout the book, you will soon discover the power of your own heart and make it a habit of loving the self.
Michael Habernig & April Hannah; Producers of *The Path: Afterlife & The Path: Beyond the Physical*

Also by Gabriella Kortsch, Ph.D.

Books:

Rewiring the Soul: How Your Connection to Yourself Can Make All the Difference

The Tao of Spiritual Partnership: Background Music in Daily Life That Can Enhance Your Growth

4-Hour Audio CD Programs

Relationships:
Priceless Tools for Self-Understanding, Growth, and Inner Freedom

Fatherless Women and Motherless Men:
The Influence of Absent Parents on Adult Relationships

Coming Soon (A Novel)

The Master Calls a Butterfly

The Power of Your Heart

Loving the Self

Gabriella Kortsch, Ph.D.

Copyright 2013 © by Gabriella A. Kortsch

All rights reserved. No part of this publication may be reproduced, stored in a retrieval system, or transmitted ion any form or by any means, electronic, mechanical, photocopying, recording or otherwise, without the prior permission of the copyright owner. The information in this book is not meant to diagnose or treat any individual or disease, and cannot be used in place of medical or psychological care.

Pages 52-54: Excerpts from *Selfishness and Self Love* by Erich Fromm. Copyright © 1939 by Erich Fromm. Reprinted by permission of Dr. Rainer Funk, Literary Executor of Erich Fromm.

Cover Design by Ignacio Martel

Library of Congress Cataloging-in-Publication Data

Kortsch, Gabriella

The Power of Your Heart: Loving the Self / Gabriella Kortsch.

Includes biographical references and index.

ISBN-13: 978 – 1492219804

ISBN-10: 1492219800

1. Spiritual life 2. Self-love 3. Love 4. Happiness 5. Wisdom 6. Mental Healing I. Kortsch, Gabriella II. Title

2013915629

First Edition

You are love.
You come from love.
You are made by love.
You cannot cease to love.

Hazrat Inayat Khan

Contents

10. Recognizing the Treasure   229

The State of Your Inner Energy
Endless Choice: It's In *Your* Hands
Bliss: Knowing You Can Always Be in a State of
Well-Being
Freedom: The Brilliant Light of Dawn

Chapter 1

The Dark Night of Anguish

Your task is not to seek for Love, but merely to seek and find all the barriers within yourself that you have built up against it.
Rumi

My greatest desire for you - and my reason for writing this book - is that you begin walking down the road to loving yourself. It is your right to live a life of love. It is also your right to understand that loving yourself *first* is not a selfish way of behavior at all, but one that allows you to live that life of love. However, it's highly probable that you never got the instruction manual explaining exactly how to accomplish this. Possibly your family - and it may well have been a loving family - considered loving the self an act of selfishness. Or perhaps the members of your family simply didn't practice loving the self, or didn't *know how* to love the self, and of course, what you didn't see - what was not modeled for you - while you were growing up, meant that you just didn't learn how to apply it to yourself. The closer you are able to move towards loving yourself, the closer you will be to living a life of love - quite independently of whether you are in a love relationship or not. A life of love can be lived with or without a partnership, because a life of love implies that you know that it all begins with *you* by loving the Self. The more clearly you understand how to love yourself, the more clearly you will see that it is very hard - if not impossible - to love others in ways that are unrelated to fulfilling needs of some kind - your needs - and that is never the healthiest way of loving, unless you first love yourself. Loving yourself first is - for so many of us - one of the hardest things we will ever learn how to do. But know this: the benefits affect you in every particle of your being - body, mind, and soul - and once you begin to do it, are greater than you will ever be able to imagine. *

*For a brief definition about the use of *self* and *Self* throughout this book, please see Appendix E.

The Deepest Pain

If there is one single thing that lies beneath all the pain, frustration, torment, anguish, doubt, fear, and stress (among others) that drives people to consult with someone such as myself, it is that they have not learned how to love the self. Almost all issues and problems that individuals tell me about contain at their most fundamental level a lack of self-love and a formidable lack of knowledge regarding how to go about accomplishing this. Indeed, so little importance is given to the possibility that a lack of self-love is paramount in resolving a psycho-emotional or spiritual issue, that many clients initially firmly reject such a suggestion. Moreover, the fact that it might be such a relatively simple solution that could offer succor seems even more improbable because we've been trained to believe that problems of this nature are hard to solve, and while I'm not suggesting that loving the self is simplistic, I *am* suggesting that simple solutions may be of greater value than we suspect.

Not loving the self, or simply not knowing about the importance of loving the self, or never having learned to love the self results in some of the most profound pain a human being can experience. You may believe that the pain of loss, abuse, abandonment, or disloyalty is the deepest pain, and in some sense you are right. But you see, it is precisely by *not* loving the self, or not knowing *how* to love the self, that the other kinds of pain just enumerated, manage to assume an iron grip on our hearts and so many other aspects of our well-being, because if we *did* love the self, or if we knew *how* to love the self, we would be able to care for the self in such a way that those other kinds of pain would be much less overwhelming.

People I see in my practice who tell me of their pain due to this or that situation in their lives (and we all have pain somewhere in our past, or even our present), some of whom are suffering in ways I would wish for no one to experience, generally believe that their suffering can only end if the person they have lost (to death, or because a relationship has ended, or because someone lives very far away and circumstances do not permit easy travel) could somehow return, or if something that occurred in the past (cruelty, abuse, etc.) could be undone by the perpetrator, and often especially, if only the whole world could understand how great their pain is (that is why they tell so many people about it in such detailed and intimate fashion), then they might feel better. Again, loving the self can alleviate such pain - not by covering it up or by somehow pretending the bad or difficult things did not happen, but by consciously taking on the responsibility for *caring* for the self in healthy ways.

Such deep and desperate pain can literally ruin your life. And of course, this is not something that depends on your socio-economic status, or on age, race, gender, profession, education, etc., but on whether you have at some point recognized that a lack of loving the self, or a *deficient* form of loving the self, can be as noxious to the health of your psyche, as a lack of vitamins or minerals to your organism. Once recognized, you can go on to remedy the situation, but until it *is* recognized, and until it is understood that no one can do this for anyone else (i.e., you have to do it for yourself), nothing will change at the root of the matter.

Furthermore, by not loving the self, or by loving the self insufficiently, and hence not caring for the self in necessary ways, the external love that enters your life - love from others - may often be tainted in some fashion. By this I don't necessarily mean that the others are lacking or wanting, but that precisely your own lack of self-love will frequently sabotage this love that enters your life from the outside - not to mention, of course, that it also means that you tend to attract a *lesser*, if you like, or more *complicated* love into your life, in order for it to allow you to learn and grow through the drama or turbulence or pain or frustration such a relationship will generally provide you with (for a discussion in much greater detail about this latter aspect, see *The Tao of Spiritual Partnership*).

> Most of the shadows of this life are caused by
> standing in one's own sunshine.
> Ralph Waldo Emerson

So the result is that pain that forms part of the tapestry of a lifetime for someone who has not learned to love the self may permeate absolutely every aspect of that life. It's a subjacent and continually underlying murmur. It never stops. Of course there are individual permutations, but imagine how a professional victory feels without a healthy dose of self-love. Doesn't it make sense that such a person will rapidly find a reason to downplay it? Or to self-denigrate? Or to rapidly need another "fix" because without it he doesn't feel good? Or, conversely, to self-aggrandize, which is simply another mask for a lack of self-love. Puffing the self up has to come from a place of lack, a place of belief that you are not good enough, not powerful enough, not intelligent enough, not rich enough, not young enough, not important enough, not - you fill in the blank - and evidently, such lack of belief in the self (which equates to lack of love of the self), will *always* create pain on a deep, primal, inner level that the person so affected is often at pains to attempt to explain, and frequently finds no explanation.

Or imagine how a moment of exquisite joy is frequently overshadowed by doubt: doubt of the self, doubt of your value, doubt of how real this moment can truly be (if you are in doubt with regard to your value), or how long it can possibly last (as it may not truly be *real*, says that self-doubting voice in the background), etc. This is pain of a most toxic and self-sabotaging kind that only we ourselves can take care of. It will never leave us thanks to another's love (although that may help for a time), and it will never leave us *just because*. If only things were so easy. It requires the recognition that the self needs tending, and this tending requires that we learn to love ourselves, as we might love a newborn baby, with all the tenderness and caring that accompanies such love.

Conversely, imagine how a moment of professional failure or personal rejection plays itself out to the individual who has not learned to approve of, like, respect, and regard the self. At such a time this person will be very adept at kicking him or herself, reproving, reproaching, and condemning himself. This only adds to the pain. And nothing will change, although the self-flagellation might lead to even greater striving for even greater potential results in the desperate search to feel better about the self. (It's also quite possible that one of those other means our society offers us to make us feel better will be chosen to alleviate some of the pain. These are means such as becoming a workaholic, abusing substances, extreme behavior, unsafe sex, adrenaline-charged risky physical activities, shopping, gambling, frenetic social activity, etc.). Super-achievers are often (but certainly not always) persons who need to achieve and be brilliant in some fashion in order to find a way to like, approve of, and admire themselves. Bearing in mind these are often highly intelligent individuals, it begs the question (which we will look at later in this book) *how is it possible they have not learned how to dissolve the pain in more direct ways; i.e., by learning how to love the self?*

The pain we feel as long as we have not learned to love the self is repeatedly blamed on others or on external circumstances, but just as often blamed on the self. Blaming the self and chastising the self for something we don't truly understand - or put into other words - something that lies outside the parameters of our experience, is like blaming yourself for failing an examination in a subject you have never studied. Imagine! You would immediately recognize how ludicrous such blaming is, and yet that is precisely what so many do and despair about, as long as they have no knowledge and understanding of the crucial importance of learning and practicing to love the self.

The Black Dungeon of Despair

If you are convinced that there is no hope for improving your life, no hope for things ever getting better for you, and no hope for you to ever feel better about your circumstances, then you are among a cohort of many individuals who feel the same. It has been called by some 'living lives of quiet desperation'. Many people quietly numb themselves to the inner pain by a diverse set of methods. In fact, many people believe that *this is just the way life is*. Nothing could be further from the truth!

Nevertheless the reality is that life does not seem to be a magnificent adventure at all to so many. If I were to ask that you define the inner quality of your daily life on a scale of 1-10, where 1 is deep despair and 10 is great joy, many might answer that they live around a 4.5 or 5 on that scale, and I am confident that you would agree with me, that while such a number is not suicidal, it is probably not a place at which you would *willingly* choose to live. But it's in that place, or even lower, where so many find themselves. And if you were to ask exactly how they got there, most will not necessarily have a clear answer to that question. *It just happened.* Life may indeed be a black dungeon of despair, and I am actually not referring to those millions who live in the third world with little access to food, water, education, and other basic needs, because their plight is so different from ours. And yet, right here in our developed and prosperous world, I find so much despair.

When I lived in Mexico in the 1990's I met people (and not necessarily only those whose financial, professional, and social situation was on a lower scale), who repeatedly used a phrase that became indelibly written in my heart as a symbol for lost hope: *ni modo*, which can be loosely translated as *nothing can be done*, or: *nothing will ever change*, or: *no matter what I do, I can't change circumstances*. About four years into the current global economic recession in 2012, I had the opportunity to speak to some inner-city school children in southern Spain in a medium-sized city. These young teens and pre-teens ranged from about 12 to 15 years of age, and were amazingly adamant in their expression of helplessness and hopelessness in view of their *perceived* circumstances in life. I use the word 'perceived' because it was clear to me due to the phrasing they used when expressing this to me, that the ideas and words came from their parents. Either they had overheard the message or they were being directly bombarded with the message at the dinner table or at any opportunity during their daily lives as a family. And - or so I reasoned - if they - the children - felt so helpless and hopeless, *how must the parents be feeling* in order to pass on these messages? This is a frightening and heart-breaking symbolic snapshot of a sector of society that is surely repeated across many nations.

> It is not the mountain we conquer but ourselves.
> Edmund Hillary

I had heard similar messages in Miami in the late 90's and early 00's from somewhat disenfranchised inner-city older teens in prevention studies in which I participated. But the message - in some format or another - also came through loud and clear in the 80's when I lived in Spain during a time when it was booming from people who very occasionally sat back to take a breath and look at their roller coaster lives, and said '*what difference does any of it make? It's all just always the same*', in the latter half of the 70's when I lived in Houston at a time during which that city was also booming, and I now *also* hear basically the same message from so many, mainly adults split roughly 60/40 percent across the board between women and men respectively of about 25 different nationalities, and ranging in age from late teens to early 70's, who seek out my services, but who may be living what appears to be - at least from the outside - a life of prosperity and ease. Why is there also such despair present in *those* lives? Why do so many seek to hide from, or escape from their daily life of despair? What has happened to us, or better said, what may have always been happening to us, or at least to a great many of us, to bring us to this black dungeon of despair?

I speculate that in other epochs - in pre-medieval Europe, for example - an age during which feudal serfdom was the norm, where the general populace may have been living lives of the utmost misery, and even horror, from our 21st century point of view, nevertheless, because there was little to compare to, other than the manner of life of the feudal lords, and because there was little to aspire to, simply because it was not possible - or so it was thought - to escape such onerous and pitiless serfdom, belief in God and Church must have been paramount as one of the *mechanisms* that kept many going in their wretched existence.

We might continue to speculate about generations of citizens using similar coping mechanisms that involved some kind of religious belief in order to somehow deal with despair in their daily lives. Think of those cultures and races throughout history that have been persecuted, besieged, and enslaved, or that were subject to terrorism and genocide, not to mention simply those whose lives, due to lack of education, hygiene, food, and clean water, were filled with abject misery and desolation. Exactly how did they cope? When you read about some of these lives, especially when survivors of such horrific conditions recount the details of their lives, do they not often focus on the fact that they were able to get though it all thanks to their belief in some higher power?

Even today, in our modern age, many are able to tolerate conditions due to their belief in some kind of religion or spirituality that other people, who are not subject to those conditions could not tolerate, or are unable to imagine tolerating, such as, for example, a person whose parent is suffering from Alzheimer's, or a parent whose child was born with an incurable genetic disorder, or a woman whose husband was killed in the line of duty, or any number of other, rather 'everyday' examples that flood our news stories and daily papers, and that we certainly run across in our daily lives, simply because we know someone who falls into one or more of those categories.

Clearly, such a belief in God, religion, or spirituality can help to soothe an agitated heart. But what happens to those who don't entertain such a belief, or - an even more puzzling question - what happens to those who do have such a belief and who nonetheless feel deep and bottomless despair? The simple answer is: learn to love the self. The corollary to that simple answer is that it is often - but not always - precisely the religious or spiritual belief that has created or led to such difficulty in loving the self. Or it may have created a feeling of impropriety about loving the self, *as if it were a bad thing to love the self*, and we will analyze this more closely further on.

Let's examine an uncomplicated analogy that might help to understand in simple terms how we could go about this process of loving ourselves better. Are you prone to getting colds a lot? Or perhaps you have frequent headaches - not major migraines, just headaches that make life a bit miserable. Or do you often accidentally bite your tongue? That's painful. How about twisting your ankle more often than most of your friends? If any of that were true, one of the things someone might say to you is that you should take better care of yourself, because *each of them could be a symptom of something else going on inside of you,* even if merely being an indication of living too 'hastily'.

With the psyche we also have symptoms of something else going on inside of you. Here are some examples:

- You are aware of really needing someone, perhaps someone you have barely met, so it makes little sense, but nevertheless, you feel as though you are unable to breathe without this person, and you suffer dreadfully when you are without him or her.

- You have allowed people in your life to treat you in ways you know are not right - perhaps not violence or physical abuse - but they have been consistently inconsiderate, unkind, rude, hurtful, etc., and you have felt the pain of it, often in your own body, perhaps in the region of your solar plexus, heart or chest. You have also felt self-loathing for allowing it to continue, but it is still happening.

Just these two examples are *symptoms* of a lack of self-love. An individual with a healthy sense of self-love, would not - I repeat - *would not allow* any of the above.

Pay attention: if you have either of these symptoms, know that your self-love is lacking. Know that you do not respect yourself the way you could and should. Knowing this does not mean that you should heap further self-loathing on your shoulders for being like this, but that you should look at yourself kindly, in understanding of your deep inner pain, and *choose* to walk down a new road. On this road self-love will be the guide you will follow and gently, lovingly, you will change the part of yourself that does not love the self.

Poor Patterns of Learned Behavior

Not loving the self is almost invariably bound up with other issues such as poor boundaries, neediness, emotional unavailability, reactivity, lack of self-responsibility, lack of self-awareness, and a host of other patterns that arise during the early part of your life where you have not been given the appropriate tools - tools that could, in effect, be easily learned in childhood. Our modern educational system carries some of the responsibility for its heinous disregard for this subject matter and hence simply not including it in the curriculum, when it could so easily be done. This results in many problems in individual lives and outcomes over the course of a lifetime.

A brief look at some of these issues can help illustrate how they *lead to* or are *caused by* (it is indeed a vicious circle) not loving the self:

Unhealthy Boundaries: How you react when others trespass your boundaries fully determines how you feel in those situations. Does your partner raise his/her voice when he/she wants to get his own way, knowing that you always back off when a voice is raised? Does your friend stand you up at the last minute after having made a lunch date with you? Does your teenage son/daughter refuse to help with household chores? Does your aging parent look at you sadly on the one night a week you decide to go out because you also want a life since your divorce, when you decided to move back home, and now says in a low tone: "don't worry about me, dear. I'll just have a sandwich here on my own in front of the TV"?

> The greatest weapon against stress is our ability
> to choose one thought over another.
> William James

Let's just take a look at the example of the energetic vampires that exist in most of our lives. They may not drain us of our blood, but they *do drain* us of our energy and emotional well-being. Sometimes we fail to recognize them for what they are because they come in the guise of helpless - almost lovable - people that populate our lives. Occasionally we *do* recognize them but have no idea how to deal with them. And frequently we *only* recognize them when they have already spent a good amount of time draining us, as said, of our energy, both physical and psychological, as well as of our emotional well-being. Some easy-to-recognize examples are:

- The friend who calls every day to re-hash the latest drama in his/her life. You *want* to be a good friend, but you are beginning to dread the calls.
- The person with whom you had an affair who threatens to harm himself if you leave him.
- A teen who tells you that unless you help with his homework, he will fail the class (this is not about 'normal' helping, but of going above and beyond because the teen is choosing not to take any initiative).
- The friend who wants to live life through you so he wants to know every detail of your life and because you began this friendship by feeling flattered that someone wanted to know so much about you, you complied, but now, months or even years later, you feel so drained, that you just want out, but of course that makes you feel guilty.

Most of these scenarios have to do with unhealthy boundaries. And unhealthy boundaries are *always* linked to a lack of self-love. *Recognizing* the vampires is not so very hard: take a moment to notice whether you feel a tightening in your gut. Or perhaps a restriction in your chest? What about queasiness? Or perhaps uneasiness? These physical sensations in your body, as well as what follows below, which is taken from the way you feel, gives you a hint that you might be in the presence of an emotional or energetic vampire. *Remember: the way your body feels when you spend time with someone, and your feelings in the emotional sense of the word, are always indicators of something going on that you want to investigate.* It may not always mean you are faced with a person of the type I have been describing, but it certainly warrants some careful consideration both of yourself and of the other person. Here are some of the ways we feel:

- Guilty (we feel guilty as we ask ourselves how we can possibly be feeling some of the things coursing through our heart, if this person is being *so good* to us *or so helpful and hospitable*).
- Drained and sapped.
- Tired and weak.
- Unenthusiastic (or if we were enthusiastic earlier in the day, after a bit of time in their presence, our enthusiasm is gone).
- Pushed and pulled in directions you don't want to go. There are strong connections to subliminal manipulation in some instances of energetic vampires.
- You may even feel befuddled, less clear in your head, as if you had been mildly drugged.

Other kinds of relationships imply that the love we feel for another human being - whether a partner, a parent, a child, or a friend - almost always carries some kind of weight with it. It might be the weight of caring responsibility for the one you love, such as the responsibility a parent carries for a child, and probably you don't consider it a weight at all. It might be the responsibility an adult child carries for an infirm elderly parent - physical care-taking responsibility, financial responsibility, or legal responsibility in the case of neurologically degenerative illnesses. It might be the responsibility an individual carries for a partner who has been diagnosed with a terminal illness, or for one who has returned psychologically damaged after serving in a war zone. These are heavy responsibilities, but you may not consider them so, simply because you love the person you care for and because they are clearly not - under these particular circumstances - able to care for themselves.

However, loving another human being might also imply the responsibility you carry for your partner from an emotional point of view, because your partner is unable to remain strong without a great deal of input and support from you. This one might weigh a bit more heavily. It might be the responsibility you carry for your partner who is needy, who clings, who is dependent, and never seems to totally grow up. This one is another kind of responsibility that might weigh heavily. It might be the responsibility you feel for the other with regards to the other's happiness. You consider it is your responsibility to make your partner happy. This is very heavy duty responsibility! It might be the responsibility you carry for a friend who somehow never seems to make it and always needs some kind of help. This one might also weigh more heavily.

The kind of responsibility that comes about with love as referred to in the second last paragraph is, I believe, 'clean'. It may weigh heavily at times, but it forms part of life, and we accept it.

It is, however, the *other* kind of responsibility that arises with love, referred to in the next paragraph (above) that I consider 'fettered'. You take on a kind of chain or strait jacket when you tacitly agree to these kinds of responsibilities with a partner who does not carry his/her own weight psychologically and emotionally. This happens when both partners are living life unconsciously and are not aware of the dynamic they have going on between them. This smacks of poor boundaries and a lack of self-love on both sides, all of which can be improved immensely by taking steps to becoming aware. Unfettered and unchained love is so much better and is what each of us deserves. Start making different choices in your life and begin the process to become aware (and you will find more specific steps to take outlined in Chapters 2, 4 and 8).

You might say that some of these examples of poor boundaries are akin to emotional manipulation or blackmail, and indeed, poor boundaries are often close relations to those behaviors. What is crucial to your own health and well-being, is how you react and what consequences you set once you begin to work with your boundaries, and in particular, what you then say or do, once that process is set in motion, should your boundaries be once again trespassed. This too, is part of learning to love and care for the self.

Neediness & Emotional Unavailability: Does the mere idea of being emotionally vulnerable with another individual scare you so much that you retreat as fast as your racing heart will permit in order to find another person who feels safer to you because they do not bring out your emotional vulnerability? This is one of the telltale signs of emotional unavailability, an issue that basically describes someone whose connection to his or her own emotions is thin, if not totally lacking. Such a person fears emotions not only in him or herself, but also those of others. We could speculate that emotions for such a person are like a foreign language that so many others know how to speak, but he does not. And because emotions create such inner havoc, this person will retreat from them, but in so doing, attract into his or her life *precisely* those people who tend to be needy or have poor boundaries, and in some fashion are the ones who will *most* push the emotionally unavailable person's buttons. This particular pattern of learned behavior is not the easiest to understand.

If you are unaware of the fact that the healthiest way to fulfill your emotional needs is by first *caring for yourself*, then you will forever be condemned to fulfill them via others. And that is not only how you (we) get into trouble, but how we become enslaved to our need for others in our life to behave in specific ways so that we can get those needs fulfilled and therefore feel good. If your partner, for example, is in a bad mood one day, if you have not yet figured out how to take care of yourself and fulfill your own needs, that bad mood will throw your day (and how you feel inside) into a tailspin and consequently threaten to curtail any chance you have at feeling good *until your partner is once again in a better mood*. Why? Because you will assume the bad mood is somehow connected to you. How you feel - under such circumstances where you are not yet loving yourself and taking good care of yourself - is indelibly intertwined with your partner's moods and behaviors, and hence you depend on your partner to be in a good place in order for you to feel good. Is there anything positive about that? Would it not make more sense that you take care of how you feel without relying on anyone else? But that requires learning how to love the self.

Have you ever had a date with someone who was rather nice, and who seemed to like you a lot as well, even going so far as saying that seeing you again would be a pleasure, but you heard no more until several weeks later? And then suddenly you found missed calls, text messages, even, perhaps, some flowers, and finally you met again for another date which again turned out to be as enchanting, if not more, as your first date. He/she continued calling, you saw each other another three or four times in succession - clearly, you had hit it off, and then, just as suddenly as this particular and exciting *hurricane* had arisen, it subsided again. This time, however, compared to the earlier, solitary date, you feel upset. Nervous, perhaps, as well, worried about - as is to be expected - *why on earth have I not heard from him/her*? You've tried to get in touch with no results, your calls go to voice mail, your texts remain unanswered. And then, a week later, it starts up again. You have another couple of great meetings, and during the third, you are blithely informed that a trip is coming up, it had been planned since before you met, and so your new person of interest will be gone for several weeks, hiking in the Himalayan lowlands. You begin to get the feeling that you are *so much more into this* than the other person, who somehow seems to stand slightly aloof of it all, and you wonder what is going on.

And of course what *is* going on is a case of mixed messages. You are being told - when the other person seeks out your company assiduously and perhaps even fervently - that you are sought after, and then - after only a short period - you get the *other* message: *what did you say your name was? Have we met?*

About two weeks after the trip to the Himalayas was over, you get a call again expressing great interest in seeing you, and indicating that he/she just knows how fascinated you will be to hear about everything that happened on the trip. *And by the way, I was thinking about you in Nepal and so I brought you an antique carved prayer bracelet from there.*

You feel pushed and pulled and you are also beginning to feel rather annoyed, perhaps even resentful. But curiously, you make few moves to confront your slippery friend, and fewer still to have a serious talk with yourself that this can't possibly be *healthy*.

So again, what is really going on?

Your new-found partner of sorts, whom you have now been seeing for several months dancing to the on-off rhythm I've described, is, of course, behaving in a way that those of you who have already shored up your listing boundaries to a healthy degree, will recognize as being unacceptable. This is the conduct of an emotionally unavailable person who does not have a healthy connection with his/her own emotions, and hence has difficulty with the emotions of others. Not only may he/she not have a healthy connection to his own inner emotions, but *there may not be any connection to them at all*. Why this is so, what happened in his life early on to make it so, is the topic for another book (although it's discussed in some detail in *The Tao of Spiritual Partnership*), but what occurs now - with you - is what concerns me here. By keeping you on stand-by mode with this on-off behavior, this person does not need to talk to you of his/her intentions. It is more than likely that there is *at least* one other person being dealt with in similar fashion, if not more, at the same time as you. You are *all* kept dangling, so to speak, by the recurring and overt interest expressed in you, then you are discarded like a toy one has grown bored with, until the interest pops up again. By not expressing his/her *real* intentions, you are kept in the dark, in suspense, but at the same time, you are kept interested enough, chafing at the bit, so to speak, so that you won't give up. The reason this person needs to do this (whether consciously or subconsciously) is because this way he/she is always emotionally *safe*. Should you, by any chance, get tired of it and leave, there is, as said, at least one other egg in the basket, perhaps several. The reason this offers emotional safety, is because this way the person who is keeping you dangling never needs to speak openly to you about how he/she feels, hence never needs to feel vulnerable, and hence no matter what happens on your side; no matter what *you* decide, he/she always has another proverbial lap to fall into. This kind of person *attracts people like you and you are attracted to people like this*. This is one of the faces of emotional unavailability.

Now: what about you? *Why are you in this situation?* Why did you not take off and leave this person weeks, if not months ago, once you began to see what was happening? Isn't it true that by the second time you spent several 'dates' together a part of you had already bonded to this person? Isn't it true that a part of you already felt the need for him/her, which you then translated into some version of great attraction or even love? And isn't it also true that you either decided you would be able to change him/her, or that he/she would change of his/her own accord upon realizing how *good* the two of you are together? *This is your clue. It's your red flag.*

Here is what you are doing: instead of looking after *yourself*, instead of questioning a person who plays (even if it's a subconscious game and not one done deliberately and with malicious calculation) such a game with you (for *whatever* reason), instead of caring enough about yourself to question this whole scenario and ask yourself if you really want to be exposed to it - at least without first having some *real* dialogue with the other party, and instead of recognizing that you are probably following a well-trodden path that you have walked on before in your life in other relationships, you are simply *forgetting about your psychological, emotional and spiritual health and well-being* and are going ahead with this pattern once again. That simply means that you would do well to think about your boundaries and your self-love. But it also means that this person is in your life for a reason: wake up to what you are *not* doing for yourself, and by not doing it (loving yourself and taking good care of yourself), you are looking for love in the wrong places.

If you will learn to love yourself first in a *healthy* way you will begin to find your way out of this pattern. Do this for yourself and you will find the well-being you are so fervently seeking.

Lack of Self-Awareness: Imagine trying to fix the hair on the back of your head without a mirror. Or imagine trying to back your car into a tight spot without the rear view mirrors. That is just a miniscule analogy of what it is like to live your life without self-awareness. Being self-aware allows you to see yourself in the mirror of all those who play major and minor roles in your life because of how you feel around them, as well as allowing you to observe your reactions to all circumstances that you meet. Observing yourself in such a way is an important process not only in getting to know yourself better, but also crucial to your inner and outer growth. And yet I imagine you realize that the number of people who are aware of themselves is much smaller than those who are not. This - awareness of yourself - greatly influences your inner well-being and to a large degree hinges on - as do so many others of these learned behaviors - whether or not you have learned to love yourself. As you grow towards self-love, you do so in part precisely because you grow in self-awareness, and - conversely - you grow in self-awareness because you are growing towards self-love. A person who loves the self in healthy ways could *never* be unaware of the self.

Blind Reactivity vs. Choice: Is there inner well-being and freedom, peace, and joy in pouncing as soon as your buttons are pushed? Is there well-being in needing to continually show the other that you are right? Or does life offer more harmony to the individual who has learned that he always has a choice? Interestingly, the former mode of behavior is seen only with people who have not yet learned how to love the self, and the latter generally only with those who have. Not having an inner self-dialogue prior to reacting - *under any circumstances* - is tantamount to being at the beck and call of anyone and everything. It also implies not having any awareness of the self because without awareness it's nearly impossible to recognize that you do always have a choice.

Lack of Life Purpose: How many people do you know that have fallen into their profession or job simply because it seemed to be a good choice due to its professional, financial, or social benefits? Or perhaps they fell into their job because there was nothing else available for their skill set. Both alternatives - and there are numerous others - imply that little or no thought was given to what a real life purpose and meaning might be. And this *only happens* if the individual does not love the self, or hasn't been shown how to love the self early on. Does that mean you can't do it later? Of course not - it just may entail a few more challenges in finding and then implementing the life purpose into a life that has already been set on its course for some years or even decades. Loving the self and finding purpose and significance in life go hand in hand with one another.

Failing to Forgive: Not knowing how to forgive, not *wanting* to forgive, and *refusing* to forgive are all part of a pattern of behavior that simply implies greater pain. Holding on to anger, resentment and anguish signify that you have little to no chances of leaving the past behind you. Failing to forgive leaves you in a perpetual state of victimhood, of having been badly treated, abused, abandoned, or otherwise harmed and signifies that a good portion of your "now" time is lived in the past.

Forgiving is ultimately a choice that you can make and to do so is to recognize that forgiving requires intention as well as attention. If you decide to forgive, it will not happen in one fell swoop. You will need to intend it over and over again, each time you think of whatever it was that occurred, and each time you think of the perpetrator of your pain. You will also need to pay close attention to your thoughts and feelings about this, because if you don't, you will not be able to carry out the intention to forgive. If you are lax about being conscious and attentive about it, it will slip by you, and you will fall back into the well-worn grooves of not forgiving and of resenting, hurting and perhaps hating. As long as you do not forgive, you have not truly learned to love the self.

Self Responsibility: This one is hard for many, because to be truly self-responsible means to literally *choose* to take on the *conscious choice* of being responsible for absolutely everything you think, feel, say, do, and how you react to *all* others and *all* circumstances.

I've written reams about this subject on my website and blogs, and all that material is freely available, but let me just reiterate this most salient point: being self-responsible means you no longer get to blame *anyone or anything* for whatever you think and feel, nor for what you say, do, or how you react to the circumstances in question. Nor do you get to allow yourself to feel that you are the victim of those circumstances or those people and whatever they did to you. What you *do* get to do is that perhaps for the first time in your life you recognize that it is always a choice. You *choose* how you think, feel, talk, act, and react, and the choice - if it is a good one - is one that works in favor of your inner well-being, your energetic frequency, and that of the global community. I know that this is a lot to take in just like that, but keep reading and it will become clearer. It is also the choice that carries within it the amazing seed for self-love.

The Promise

Clearly, the promise of self-love, if you decide to travel down that road, is one of redemption from pain, deep despair, and anguish. It is a promise of inner well-being, of peace, of harmony, and of joy. Freedom comes with it. These promises that may not sound greatly exciting (especially to the very young), nevertheless, pledge something to those who have already traveled a portion of their life trajectory, that has become so valuable, that these individuals are willing to forego much, and be very patient - lovingly patient - with themselves, in order to achieve self-love.

Sitting on a sled at the top of a hill in late summer will not make the snow come more quickly, nor will incessantly watering a seed in the ground make the oak tree grow more rapidly, nor will opening a chrysalis help the butterfly emerge more quickly. *We know this.* You don't really need me to tell you.

But we often forget this in our own process. We want definitive results long before we have learned how to add and subtract and we want wings long before we learn how to walk, let alone run and fly. Our lives are a process of growth, sometimes slowly, sometimes in greater spurts, but immediate growth all the way takes place for almost no one. Epiphanies may happen, but what is realized in that brilliant burst of light, almost always still requires practice if you want to fully assimilate it. Remember how long Olympic contenders train and practice. Remember how long a concert pianist has lessons and endless hours of practice. So too, it is with the evolution of our selves throughout the course of our lives.

Nietzsche put it beautifully: *He who would learn to fly one day must first learn to stand and walk and run and climb and dance; one cannot fly into flying.*

Let's love ourselves enough to give ourselves time to learn how to stand and walk and run and climb and dance before we fly - but let's definitely not stop until we *do* know how to fly and thus truly love ourselves!

Consider who it is that holds the key to your happiness. Or perhaps I should ask *what* holds the key to your happiness? In the first instance, it is a specific (or more than one specific) human being that holds the key to your happiness. Perhaps it is your partner without whom you are incapable of being happy. Or perhaps your child, adult or small. Or perhaps your parent, or even a pet. In the second instance, it is a *something* that holds the key to your happiness. This can be something material, such as the balance in your bank account or portfolio, or the size and location of your home, or it could be your youth, your strength, your professional situation, your academic credentials, your social position, and so on.

In all instances, you derive your happiness from an outer source, and hence the key to your happiness lies without and not within.

Perhaps you can see the problem with that. People can let you down, leave you, or die. Material things can disappear, as can youth or professional and social positions. If any of that happens, and if the key to your happiness lies there, *then what are you going to do?*

Recognizing that happiness first needs to come from the inside out is your path out of the above dilemma. Starting to walk on that path requires conscious awareness of a desire or intention to begin to love yourself. So once again - and you will see this over and over again in this book, the more you love yourself, the more you will be able to find happiness on the inside and will notice - perhaps to your surprise - that you no longer need to find it on the outside, or at least, that you will no longer look for it on the outside.

In *Rewiring the Soul* I wrote the following: *The less you love yourself the more likely it is that you believe another holds the key to your happiness.* This book that you hold in your hands now has been written to show you how *you* can be the one to hold the key to your happiness and inner well-being by learning how to love yourself.

To be beautiful means to be yourself. You don't need to be accepted by others. You need to accept yourself.
Thich Nhat Hanh

Chapter 2

Loving the Self Defined

There is no mistaking love. You feel it in your heart. It is the common fiber of life, the flame that heats our soul, energizes our spirit, and supplies passion to our lives.
Elisabeth Kübler Ross

It makes sense that if you love someone, you care for them, you honor them, and - at least in some ways - you approve of them. Furthermore, frequently you have grown to feel this way about them over a period of time. It didn't just happen all at once, but as you came to know them and appreciate them over time. Even in the case of your children you probably loved them before they were born, but nevertheless grew to appreciate them in the way described here, as you saw the gradual unfolding of their character traits, their way of being, and behavior as they grew into childhood, adolescence, and adulthood.

That we believe that it should be any different at all with the self simply makes no sense. And so we are able to define what loving the self entails in ways that closely resemble our relationships with others, although with one rather startling and crucial caveat. We *never* love the self because of what the self gives us in the sense of fulfilling our needs from the outside. This implies psychological, emotional, and spiritual maturity. Let's examine this on the basis of a simple example.

Perhaps you recall the first time you fell in love. Probably you were still a teen. Typically, the person you fell in love with made you feel something you had never felt before. It was heady. It was exhilarating. You wanted more of that feeling, so of course you wanted to be with that person as much as possible because *being with that person* gave you that feeling. Or so it appeared. There are many possible reasons for feeling that way, but one of the most typical ones is the fact that when the other person 'loves' you back, or simply is also attracted to you the way you are to him/her, what you then see in their eyes when they look at you (apart from the chemistry that is probably swirling around the two of you in a state of perpetual excitement), is this love or attraction for you, and it is *that* which makes you feel so good. It makes you feel so good because seeing that love or attraction for you *in their eyes*, allows you, while you are with them and they are showing this love or attraction for you, *to feel the way you would if you loved yourself.* You're not conscious of this. You think you love them because they are so handsome/beautiful, intelligent, witty, proactive, sporty, etc., but what is really happening on another level is that you are - perhaps for the first time in your life - connecting with a feeling that shows you how it feels to love yourself, but on the basis of what you see in their eyes. In other words, it is dependent on them showing this love or attraction for you. It does not arise from you, but arises from what you see in their eyes. This is one of the reasons (although not the only one) why we suffer so much when someone we love stops loving us, or leaves us, or transfers their love for us to someone else. We are no longer able to feel the way we did when they loved us.

Love is the great miracle cure.
Loving ourselves works miracles in our lives.
Louise L. Hay

So coming back to the point I was making earlier: part of what we feel for this person is based on our need for what they are supplying us with: their love which allows us to feel the way we would if we loved ourselves. But when we love ourselves *consciously*, we don't do so because we 'need' ourselves, but because we are fully aware of the fact that by loving the self, we begin to supply for ourselves that which, before we became truly aware, we looked for in other people. We will come back to this point again later in this book, but this is what you need to understand for now: the more you are able to supply these needs for yourself, the more you are becoming an adult, the less you live out portions of yourself through others, and the less you need to blame others or circumstances for *anything* at all.

Loving the self implies psychological, emotional, and spiritual maturity. As we have already seen, it also implies being aware of the self, as well as being responsible for the self.

Caring

How do we care for another? Or - and this might be easier to answer, almost universal in its simplicity - how do we care for a new-born child? Do we not take every little thing that such a helpless infant requires into consideration? Do we not take it upon ourselves to ensure the safety, comfort, love, and yes - care - of this baby in all ways possible? We do not let it suffer. We do not let it get cold, or too hot. We keep it clean. We give it soft bedding. We wrap it in warm blankets. We feed it. We carry it around in our arms to lull it to sleep. We sing to it. We caress it. And if - by some strange chance - it should be hurt, or alarmed, we immediately do whatever is necessary to ensure that it regains some measure of harmony. We (most of us) do all these things and don't even think about them. We consider it normal and natural to care for a baby in such a way, and would most certainly not stop doing it - even if we were very tired, or annoyed (with our own day or life), or sad, or angry, or helpless or desperate. We would simply continue caring for that baby.

Friendship with oneself is all-important, because without it
one cannot be friends with anyone else.
Eleanor Roosevelt

When we begin to love the self, it has to be very much like that. Clearly, because we're not used to being like that with ourselves, we have to keep reminding ourselves to behave like that, and to show the same kind of loving concern and care for ourselves as we would, if we were taking care of a helpless infant. Here are some ideas to consider:

- How do you care for yourself when you are in physical pain?
- How do you care for yourself when you are in psychological or emotional pain?
- What do you do for yourself when you are feeling stressed?
- What do you do for yourself when you are tired?
- What do you do for yourself when you feel despondent or hopeless?

- What do you do for yourself when you feel angry, resentful, or bitter?
- What do you do for yourself when you don't know how to go on?
- How do you care for yourself when someone you love has just announced they are leaving you?
- How do you care for yourself when you have just received bad news from your doctor?
- How do you care for yourself when you have just lost your job?
- What do you tell yourself when you are lost (in any way at all)?
- What do you tell yourself when you need a kind word?
- What do you tell yourself when you need an encouraging word?
- Do you pay attention to yourself when you need help of any kind?

Questions such as these are a continual guide and reminder to remain aware while you are learning to love and care for yourself. If you make a habit - at least at the beginning - to ask yourself these and similar questions at every turn of the way, you will soon begin to notice when you are *not* taking good care of yourself. And at that point you can begin to proactively change these behavior patterns.

Let's look at another set of questions regarding totally different situations:

- What do you tell yourself when you served poorly at tennis?
- What do you tell yourself when your golf handicap worsens?

- What do you tell yourself when you come in near the end of the marathon you trained for all summer?
- What do you tell yourself when you fail to win the seat in your local community government?
- What do you tell yourself when you get a rejection letter from yet another agent?
- What do you tell yourself when you don't win the baking contest?
- What do you tell yourself when you begin to lose your temper (about anything at all)?
- What do you tell yourself when you notice you are becoming very impatient?
- What do you tell yourself when you are feeling jealous or envious (for whatever reason)?
- What do you tell yourself when you feel sad?
- What do you tell yourself when you feel fear?
- What do you tell yourself when you feel lonely?

In all of these situations, you ideally need some kind of encouragement and you need some kind of soothing. It's always easiest if you imagine any of these things happening to your child, or a young friend (or anyone else, for that matter), to whom you then offer support and kindness and understanding for how they feel at that moment. Or do you really see yourself saying to a young child who has been trying to learn how to play tennis, and who fails to hit the ball: *you are so stupid! How is it possible that you can never get it right??*

And yet, if you think about it, that is probably the way you speak to yourself when you fail to get something right, isn't it? Why be so mean to yourself, when you can be so kind to another? Now do you see that one of the missing elements is love? *What's missing is your love for yourself.* Once you see that, and once you begin the process towards manifesting that love *for yourself,* it will become increasingly easy to be supportive and encouraging in your inner self-dialogue.

Another set of questions that require caring - and of course, as we have seen - they also require continual aware vigilance or vigilant awareness of your thoughts and feelings is:

- What do you tell yourself when you compare your appearance to that of another person?
- What do you tell yourself when you compare your achievements to that of another?
- What do you tell yourself when you compare your home, what stands in your driveway, where you vacation, and what you wear to that of another person?
- What do you tell yourself when you feel you are less worthy than another because of any of the above comparisons?

Think for a moment how you would react if it were your teenage or adult child who was going through such a process and who comes to you feeling low and worthless because of a comparison of the above nature. Isn't it true that in the first place you would comfort him, and then encourage him, possibly point out some of the goals he has already achieved in one arena or another, indicating that the methods that were used to achieve said goals are also methods that might be used to prevail or grow further in a current situation, and so on? Additionally, you might then perhaps gently probe with some questions pertaining to whatever it is that he feels he has not fully grasped on a given level, in order to determine whether he might benefit from further education of some kind, increasing his skills in some field, etc. And of course, *this is the way you should be dialoguing with yourself on the inside,*

*when you are the one telling yourself any of the above things. This is
a crucial variable involved with what it means to begin to care for
and love the self.*

Honoring & Respecting

How do we honor someone we respect? How do we behave
around a person we honor? How do we feel about a person we
honor and respect? These are simple questions to answer because
it's so clear. What we certainly do *not* do when it concerns
someone we honor and respect, is to speak or think badly of them,
treat them poorly or disrespectfully, make rude comments in their
presence, and so on. We don't belittle them, we don't denigrate
them, we don't tell others something disparaging about them, and
we give them the benefit of the doubt when for some reason they
are being maligned and we give them a chance to take a breath and
explain what is going on.

The way you treat yourself sets the standard for others.
Sonya Friedman

So it stands to reason that when we honor and respect the
self, we need to behave in similar ways, including giving *ourselves*
the benefit of the doubt. Here are some thoughts:
- How do you talk to yourself about yourself?
- How do you think about yourself?
- How do you describe yourself to others?
- What do you say to yourself when you make a mistake?
- What do you say to others when you make a mistake?
- What do you say to yourself when you fail at something?
- What do you say to others when you fail at something?

- What do you say to yourself when someone criticizes you?
- What do you say to the person who criticizes you?

These questions show very clearly the areas of difficulty for an individual who does not honor and respect the self. What you say to yourself and the manner in which you dialogue with yourself in any of the above examples, and how you then speak to others in those situations, tells you a great deal about the degree to which you honor and respect yourself. To begin with, as already clearly mentioned in all the other sections of this chapter, without awareness of the self, or without being conscious, loving the self, and also honoring and respecting the self, is not possible. You need to be aware in order to *catch* the habitual, non-loving, non-caring, non-respectful and non-honoring thoughts as they enter your mind, in order to countermand them with another kind of dialogue: a loving and caring one. It may simply be that you seek to regain a measure of inner balance before going on with the next part of the self-dialogue, but wanting to do that, wanting to have that inner balance, is already a firm indication of the fact that you care enough about yourself to do this. It also tells us that you know that if you don't do it, you will probably go down a nasty back alley somewhere in your mind where you wind up as a piece of garbage instead of the glorious human being that you are and can be.

> When I let go of what I am, I become what I may be.
> Lao Tzu

Here is another point to consider: if you honor and respect yourself, *you will honor your process of growth*, fully including in that honoring and respecting mistakes and failures that may occur along the way. You honor and respect the process of knowing and achieving knowledge and experience, you honor and respect that you are even on such a path, and it is in your awareness of yourself and your process, that you are able to observe with love and care the steps that you take in order to 'grow' yourself; in order to become more of what you may be.

This process of growth is also addressed below in the section on finding a meaning or purpose in your life because as you do so, you begin to recognize that even when you are still far away from what might be called a true life purpose, you need to honor and respect the steps you are taking in that direction, although those steps may not look like a *purpose* at all.

All the parts that define what loving the self means are so inter-connected and intertwined, that if one is being recognized and worked on, or if you are attempting to improve one, *all others* will also be affected.

Approving & Admiring

When you love the self, you consciously and joyously approve of and admire yourself when that is appropriate and deserved. But conversely, when approving yourself and admiring yourself is not deserved, because you are aware that you have been participating in behavior that is less than exemplary, you nevertheless continue to love the self, as a loving parent continues to care for and love the recalcitrant or misbehaving child. You don't shout at yourself, you don't criticize yourself, but you do look at yourself with evermore aware eyes in order to change whatever behavior or way of thinking or reacting it is that you recognize as not being something that will move you into this path of healthy and aware self-love that you have chosen. When you consciously love the self, you know that admiration and approval of yourself is healthy and that it stimulates greater love for others around you, as well as a greater capacity to draw behavior from others that will allow them to come closer to approving of and admiring themselves. *Your light allows others to see their own light.*

It's easy to think of how we approve of or admire certain people. Often these are individuals who have some status, perhaps celebrities, or also those who, while not well-known, may have accomplished something very specific in their field, a scientist, an artist, a composer, a poet, a small town architect, etc. Perhaps the person we admire is the fireman who marches bravely into a burning home in order to save the children that are inside, or the teacher at the inner-city school who buys supplies with her own money so that the students can work with them. Perhaps the person we approve of and admire is someone who was injured in an accident and nevertheless has not only picked up their life by the threads, but is now competing in paralympic sports, or giving motivational talks to others who are similarly affected. Or perhaps it's someone who lost all their money and is now building up another life for themselves and their family.

> Love is but the discovery of ourselves in others,
> and the delight in the recognition.
> Alexander Smith

Nevertheless, when it comes to approving of and admiring ourselves, we tend to fail dismally. As we have seen, there are several important reasons for this:

- we weren't taught how to do it
- we believe if we do it, we are boasting and bragging
- we are our own worst critics and hence find it hard to admit that we have done something well enough to admire it and approve of it

- we believe it's in bad taste
- we may also hear the voice of a critical parent in our heads

Let's examine some of the ways we react with ourselves when we've done something that others might approve of or admire in us:

- How do you react verbally when someone compliments you on your clothing or appearance?
- How do you react on the inside, with your self-talk when someone compliments you on what you are wearing or other aspects of your appearance?
- How do you react verbally when someone compliments you on something you have done?
- How do you react on the inside, with regards to your self-talk when someone compliments you on something you have done?
- What do you say to yourself when you have completed a goal you set out to do: on the job, at home, in sports, etc.?
- How do you react verbally when you have done something you consider well-done, and someone criticizes or belittles it?
- Finally, how do you react on the inside, with your self-talk when you have done something you consider well-done, and someone criticizes or belittles it?

Let's go back to those people we approve of or admire. When someone criticizes them, or what they have done, how and to what degree is your reaction different than your reaction when *you* are the one being criticized? In the case of the person you admire, are you steadfast in your admiration of him? When you are the one being criticized, do you feel something disintegrate inside of you as you hear the damning words?

Think back! How many times have you felt your resolve crumbling when you are not held up on a pedestal? Is your approval and admiration of yourself strong enough (assuming that what you have done deserves it) to withstand harsh words, looks that belittle and denigrating reactions of any kind? Careful - I'm not talking about refusing to see potential areas for improvement and blindly believing that anything that comes from you is worth gold. Rather, I'm talking about you knowing you have done good work. You can compare your work to others and see its value. Can you, in instances of that nature, maintain your resolve about the quality of your work if others criticize or judge it?

Let's use an even simpler example. You've taken a liking to someone. You met at a party. You see that person again on another occasion, and knowing yourself to be looking good, that day you approach him/her in order to suggest meeting over the weekend for dinner. You get a cool look in response and a refusal. Now what? *Exactly what happens to your inner admiration and approval rating?*

These are not easy moments for anyone. Rejection doesn't exactly fuel self-approbation. But here's the thing: if you truly do admire yourself (in a healthy way), and if you truly do approve of yourself, the rejection by a stranger will not change that. Loving yourself takes care of those typical dives on the self-approval rating, because if you love yourself you know your true value, and if you know your true value, it will not unravel because someone else doesn't want to have dinner with you. Part of what happens is that your self-dialogue kicks in. Of course you're not going to hop for joy when you've been rejected. Nor will you pretend to yourself that it's not affecting you, because depending on where you find yourself on your path towards self-love, it may still affect you enormously. But as said, your inner dialogue will kick in, and you will begin by reassuring yourself that your value has not diminished because one individual prefers not to have dinner with you. Perhaps he/she prefers blondes, or darker skin, or someone younger, older, thinner, heavier, you name it, because at this point, that individual knows next to nothing about you and is basing their refusal on any number of factors that have little or nothing to do with you because they don't know you (And all you know about them is that you felt a certain attraction). Further, you will reassure yourself in this inner dialogue that your value has not diminished by being rejected just in the same way paper money does not lose its value if someone throws it away, or steps on it, or loses it. You reassure yourself in this inner dialogue *because you love yourself.* You care about yourself, you respect and honor yourself, and you approve of and admire yourself. For all these reasons you do not allow a rejection to cause you to consider your value has changed one iota.

Seeking Your Purpose

It is difficult, if not impossible to imagine an individual who has learned to love the self, who does not have a purpose or meaning in his life. Having such a purpose brings joy, fulfillment, satisfaction, and a sense of accomplishment to everyone who has found it, but it also brings an added benefit: it acts - that is, having a purpose in your life - acts in times of need and distress as an oak tree inside of you that holds you up and supports you, precisely because of how much it means to you.

Another important element of seeking and having a purpose in your life is that it connects you to a part of you that you may not be very familiar with. Your *inner Self,* the part of you that occasionally tries to speak with you via intuition or dreams, and that you most likely pay scant attention to, but also the part of you that is eternal and will never die, and that has always been, *that part of you* resonates with certain things. In other words, there is a *quickening* in you when, for example, you see a documentary on television that may be connected in some fashion to what might someday become your purpose. If you *notice* this quickening (because you are practicing being aware) and if you know what it *means* (because you understand that you need to pay close attention when your body reacts in some way to an external stimulus), then you will also *know* that you owe it to yourself (because you love yourself and care for yourself) at the very minimum to further explore whatever it is that is creating a resonance in you. You might feel this resonance or quickening as a kind of butterfly sensation in your solar plexus, or an excitement of sorts, a shortness of breath (in the good sense), or in any other way that you would classify as positive. Examine this.

> We are each gifted in a unique and important way. It is our privilege and our adventure to discover our own special light.
> Mary Dunbar

Loving yourself and caring for yourself means that you are not willing to spend your life simply doing something because it allows you to make a good living. Obviously if what you are doing does fulfill you and gives you a sense of purpose, then you're already there, but this is most definitely not the case with many people. When I was quite young, I read about people who led lives of *quiet desperation* and although I was still at an early stage of my own life, I shuddered at the images that expression evoked in me and vowed that I would never live such a life.

I didn't know then what I know now, but I always had a sense of adventure somewhere inside of me when I thought of doing certain things with my life. That sense of adventure and excitement was very strong in my teens, then suddenly I paid less attention to it, gave it scarcely any attention at all, until one fine day, somewhere in my late 20's, I realized I hadn't felt it for a long time. It seemed to have gotten lost in the shuffle. Or perhaps I had lost my way. Whatever it was, I felt devastated that I couldn't feel it - find it - anymore, and so I set out to see what I could do, thinking that if I couldn't regain it, life simply meant so much less and contained so much less joy and anticipation. This had nothing to do with the circumstances of my life: my family, children and other details, as much as an element inside of me that seemed to have gone astray. I had lost it, I feared, and I dreaded having a life without it.

So I began reading more of what I had been reading in those teenage years when I felt the sense of adventure (see many of the books listed in the Bibliography of this book in your hands), and it seemed to me that slowly the sense of adventure returned, although at that time I could never quite grasp it. I wasn't quite sure what it was trying to tell me, and I didn't have someone like myself to encourage me to listen to what my body was telling me, or to observe how I reacted when I watched certain programs or documentaries on television, when I read a certain kind of book, or heard conversation about certain subjects, and so on.

At any rate, if you care about yourself, you will give this some very serious consideration. A life without a purpose or meaning that fulfills you in some way and that is not dependent on people in your life, is a life that is missing one of its most fundamental elements. If your life purpose is your family or your partner or your children, while those are arguably some of the most important parts of our lives, I would venture to say that in that case you have not yet really found your true purpose, because your purpose needs to emanate from you, as opposed to being dependent on a relationship with others.

Start by observing yourself closely, as said, for tell-tale signs of quickening or excitement when certain subjects or fields of interest cross your path. Pay close attention and examine how these might connect to something deep within you that is calling for your consideration. Perhaps there are threads that connect this interest to something that will lead you to your purpose, or perhaps you need to become a detective and find the links in order to understand why this particular topic creates a reaction in you. If none of that rings a bell, try to remember what it was that you dreamed of around puberty. What was it that you wanted to do or become? Perhaps there you will find something that takes you down the path to your life meaning. You can also make a list of all the things that you *know* are *not* the ones, eliminating them, and that leaves you with another list of potentials. Go down that list gently, slowly, to discover whether any parts of it cause a resonance in you. Perhaps you already have a hobby or field of study or other occupation in your spare time that speaks to you in ways that your regular work does not. In that case, you may need to figure out a way of incorporating that into your life in more meaningful ways.

However you do it, understand that without it your life will never be as rich as it could be with it. This will depend on your caring and love of yourself, but as part of the process of learning to care for and love yourself, you will soon notice that this endeavor continually shows you - on subliminal levels - that you are important to you, and that, by itself, is already a huge step in the right direction.

Loving the self is partially defined by seeking your purpose. Those who give it no consideration or importance have simply not yet taken the decision to care for themselves in a way that is not only life-promoting but also that ensures a firm and staunch support in times of need. But having a path in life that means something to you goes far beyond what I've described up to now. Some would describe it as the *opus* that alchemists in other eras might have spent an entire lifetime on in order to transform, for example, coal to gold. Those alchemists talked about the *nigredo* or blackness, Jung and his disciples spoke of the *shadow* aspect of the psyche, and what it all comes down to is facing those parts of yourself that are not necessarily brilliant. In fact, those unrecognized parts of you may be so deep in shadow, that you are not even aware of them. In this sense, what you do with your life, over the course of your entire trajectory - even during the part in which you had no idea that perhaps there was a higher purpose to your life - you do in order to transform yourself in similar fashion. Your entire life can be likened to that *opus*.

So of course you have to go about it trial and error. You are not going to get it right the first time, perhaps not even the 51st or 178th time, but you *are* going to continue - once you decide that loving and caring for yourself is part of what you do - because you realize it is not so much about getting it right, as about continuing on this path towards your blossoming, evolving, and persistent growth. You are a constant work in progress and you will soon come to realize that all you do along this path, and every step you take in one direction or another, is simply part of that which illuminates aspects of yourself. And your goal, of course, is to illuminate the whole. And the method by which you do this is by moving towards your purpose, towards that which gives you meaning, towards that with which you resonate on that deep, inner, divine level.

The Selflessness of Self-Love

Self-love is selfless - for a fully conscious human being - because to love the self is to know that by loving the self all others will be more fully loved by the self. Read that again: *to love the self is to know that by loving the self all others will be more fully loved by the self*. Why? Because only by loving the self can we even begin to hope to understand what it means that we are all one, and that if I love one I love all, and if I love all, I am capable of loving any one of the all. *We are all one.*

For many people, that is a total conundrum, contradiction, and impossible to understand. To love others, I must love them first, they say, and I should be selfless. If I love myself first, I am being selfish!

This fallacy has been propagated by our culture for centuries, if not millennia. Our religions and those who speak on behalf of our religious institutions, our philosophers, our educational systems, and our very own ideas about parenting and loving - to name only a few - lie at the bottom of this tremendously harmful way of thinking. It leads to people not learning to love themselves, to not knowing how to love themselves, to feeling guilty if they ever do, and to propagating the same miserable *modus operandi* with the next generation.

This will be more fully discussed in Chapter 3, but now I'd like to point out something so elementary, and yet so evocative of what this business of *loving the self* first is really all about.

> To be yourself in a world that is constantly trying to make you
> something else is the greatest accomplishment.
> Ralph Waldo Emerson

You know that when you travel by air, prior to take-off a cabin attendant walks you through the safety procedures. One of the things they stress for all passengers is the fact that if barometric pressure were to fall, oxygen masks will drop in front of everyone's face. They encourage those passengers traveling with children to *put their own masks on first* and only then help their children. Why? Because having ensured their own well-being, these parents are now able to ensure the well-being of their children. If they had *not* ensured their own well-being by putting on their own masks first, they might well lose consciousness due to the lack of oxygen and then where would the children be with no one left to take care of them?

This is an important analogy to consider very, very carefully. That parent is not being selfish. Quite the contrary. The parent who *takes care of him or herself first* by strapping on his own mask first ensures the well-being of his children. *He cares for himself first in order to be able to care of others.*

It's the same story with loving the self. By taking good care of yourself first by ensuring that you know how to keep yourself in a state of inner well-being (which is essentially saying the same as loving yourself), you will be in a position to be able to help others in ways you could not, if you were not taking care of yourself. By not loving yourself first, just like the parent in the airplane who would lose consciousness, you might lose your awareness of what a situation is all about and become reactive, or start projecting, or move into a non-adult, child-like state emotionally, simply because you had not yet begun the process of loving yourself. Let's be clear, loving yourself obviously does *not* mean that you have all the answers. It just means that your inner state is almost always in a place from where it's easier to be non-reactive, aware, self-responsible, and to recognize that you always have a choice.

Being Vigilant

Being vigilant is another way of thinking about being aware. You see, if you want any of the behaviors we're discussing here to become an integral part of your life, you simply can't stop being vigilant. It's essential that you remember to be aware *at all times*. So you've got to be vigilant about being aware. At the beginning this will not come easily or naturally at all. You will find yourself falling back into old habits, and particularly losing track of present time by following strands of random thought into netherworlds that take you to places of pain and darkness. Those thoughts appear in part because you have stopped being vigilant about being aware, and in part because you have such strong neural pathways associated with those ways of thinking.

If you are depressed you are living in the past. If you are anxious you are living in the future. If you are at peace you are living in the present.
Lao Tzu

So you need a mechanism to remind you. One (that I refer to in all my books) is simply sticking some post-it's in obvious places in your home and office (bathroom mirror, fridge, laptop screen, etc.) that say 'what am I thinking?', or 'what am I feeling?', or that have a quote you like but you know it's meant to remind you to focus on what you are thinking or feeling *in order to move away from that blind - and automatic - mode you had fallen into and to then regain control of those thoughts and feelings.* Doing this several times during the day, every day, will soon create a habit of greater and greater awareness at all times.

Another mechanism to help you is the Gratitude Exercise found in Appendix A, and the Mindfulness Walk found in Appendix B. We'll talk more about these later. In the meantime, simply remember that being vigilant about your thoughts and feelings is part of how we can define loving the self.

Chapter 3

Why the Self is Not Loved

We are wont to condemn self-love; but what we really mean
to condemn is contrary to self-love. It is that mixture of selfishness
and self-hate that permanently pursues us, that prevents us from
loving others, and that prohibits us from loving ourselves.
Paul Valéry

The question why the self is not loved automatically, so to speak, is one that has puzzled many. We are born as innocents - would we know how to love ourselves without so much pondering on the subject if we were raised away from the impact of our culture, our religions - organized and otherwise - and if those who raised us had also been raised in such a way? Obviously it's impossible to say since we can't recreate such circumstances, but we can be quite certain that much of what has run amok with our natural capacity for self-love is what comes at us in the guise of all those who surround us, beginning with those who stood directly next to our cribs, and reaching all the way out to those ubiquitous billboards that tell us you are beautiful at the same time as they encourage us to nip and tuck our flesh, purportedly in order that we can be as beautiful (and hence worthy of our love) as they tell us we supposedly are.

The underlying message, of course, is that we are not good enough the way we are. That is insidious. And we're not even aware of it. But if we're not good enough, how can we love ourselves? Such a billboard or glossy magazine message is merely the tip of the iceberg and - at least for now - affects women much more than men, but we can see it all around us, it's often subliminal and it's so terribly ubiquitous. The internet - wonderful though it is, and I thank my good fortune to have been born in this epoch - brings it to everyone. Residents in the favelas in Rio want brand name sneakers. Why? It raises their value in their eyes and in the eyes of so many of their peers. Citizens of nations that are barely surfacing from hunger and poverty want external emblems of something that will give them recognition because they so erroneously believe that they will be worth more by having whatever 'it' is and hence will be able to love themselves or respect or approve of themselves more. In some fashion much of the world feels the same way. Individuals who have made fortunes in growing economies such as China and Russia flock to Europe and America to buy something, to buy whatever, because in their eyes - and in ours - that something raises their value. Why else would we spend so much of our time and energy watching programs on television that talk endlessly about subjects such as these, or that show us what this person or that person has? We equate external possessions and power with personal value. And it's from there where we then most frequently obtain our ideas about how to love the self. We have become so immured against natural thinking - in so many ways, not just those that are rather more obvious such as the ones just described - that many people haven't a clue that they truly may and can - not to mention could and should - love themselves. What they know and understand even less is the benefit such self-love will bring not only themselves, but also all those whose lives they touch.

In the following sections of this chapter we will examine some of the obstacles to loving the self.

The *Selfishness* of Self-Love

Loving yourself is selfish. *We get that.* It's understood. We've heard it in some version or another since childhood. We never question the contradiction to that statement in this one: *love thy neighbor as thyself.* It's a gross contradiction because if it is selfish to love myself, then it is in some fashion also selfish - in other words not good - to love my neighbor, right? Or - and this is the way most seem to wind up understanding it - we are meant to love our neighbor first, and only then (perhaps) love ourselves. So there is this dichotomy of concepts that seems to fill our mind with doubt and our heart - should we dare to put ourselves first (in the healthy, self-loving way) - with guilt, because, after all, it is selfish to love ourselves first.

Dedicate yourself to Love. Decide to let Love be your intention, your purpose, and your point. And then let Love inspire you, support you and guide you in every other dedication you make thereafter.
Robert Holden

Time and time again I hear participants in my workshops, or attendees at my talks, or clients in my private practice saying that even just *speaking* about loving themselves, not to mention loving themselves *first*, makes them feel extremely uncomfortable. In fact, some timidly venture that it might be a *sin.* Such thinking only happens if you've been brain-washed in some fashion about the concept of self-love. And of course one of the brain-washing mechanisms has to do with the idea - so alive in our current cultural climate - that loving the self is selfish.

In an earlier book: *Rewiring the Soul,* I addressed this issue extensively and reproduce here some paragraphs from that book:

Much of this has its origin in the somewhat erroneous or skewed interpretation of scripture by the bastions of most organized religions, as well as ideology, philosophy, and ethics. To illustrate this point, I will repeat here something I have already written about in the past, but which is very illuminating about the topic. It comes from Erich Fromm, the author of *The Art of Loving* in his 1939 article titled *Selfishness and Self-Love:*

"Modern culture is pervaded by a taboo on selfishness. It teaches that to be selfish is sinful and that to love others is virtuous. To be sure, this doctrine is not only in flagrant contradiction to the practices of modern society but it is also in opposition to another set of doctrines which assumes that the most powerful and legitimate drive in man is selfishness and that each individual by following this imperative drive also does the most for the common good. The existence of this latter type of ideology does not affect the weight of the doctrines which declare that selfishness is the arch evil and love for others the main virtue. Selfishness, as it is commonly used in these ideologies, is more or less synonymous with self-love. The alternatives are either to love others which is a virtue or to love oneself which is a sin."

We have been socialized into believing that if we profess to love the self, we are being selfish. *Nothing could be further from the truth!* To understand this better, let's look at some definitions of selfishness: self-centeredness, egotism, state of only having concern for one's own self. But *loving the self does not preclude having concern for others*, it simply means that you take care of yourself first, in order to be able to take care of or have concern for others *better than if you had not taken care of yourself first.*

A case in point, that I often use to illustrate this with my clients, are the instructions given by airline personnel when they show passengers the use of the oxygen mask. In the case of need, they say, if you are traveling with children, *put your own mask on first* (so that you don't run the risk of falling unconscious before you can help them). In other words: *take care of yourself first.* Most people upon hearing this simplistic analogy get it immediately and recognize that there is not one iota of selfishness in the act of loving the self first.

Fromm becomes even more damning as he continues his assault on our societal mores concerning self-love:

"The doctrine that selfishness is the arch-evil that one has to avoid and that to love oneself excludes loving others is by no means restricted to theology and philosophy. It is one of the stock patterns used currently in home, school, church, movies, literature, and all the other instruments of social suggestion. "Don't be selfish" is a sentence which has been impressed upon millions of children, generation after generation. It is hard to define what exactly it means. Consciously, most parents connect with it the meaning not to be egotistical, inconsiderate, without concern for others. Factually, they generally mean more than that. "Not to be selfish" implies not to do what one wishes, to give up one's own wishes for the sake of those in authority; i.e., the parents, and later the authorities of society."

Please read the foregoing paragraph again because for those of you who disagreed with my earlier statements regarding theology, philosophy, and ethics because we are no longer living in the Middle Ages, or because your family did not go to church, etc., you may have now seen glimpses of yourself in this second Fromm citation. *Not because your parents were reprehensible, but because they knew not what they did*, and anyway, they were probably the fruit of the earlier socialization by their own process of growing up as described above. But no matter how you look at it, we are again faced with the implacable wall that indicates that we are selfish if we dare do what we think is right, or what we want ... imagine the heresy ... *doing what we want* ... even if it is something like desiring to study art instead of law (which might be what father wants). Examples abound. This is also the starting point for many unhealthy boundaries in people ... unhealthy boundaries mean that the individual allows others to cross limits that should not be crossed ... all learned in childhood by learning *not to be selfish*, or by learning to *please another*. (Note: poor boundaries also have other origins).

I am confident you can understand from the above statement, that many members of generations upon generations of Christians* have learned that *to be fond of oneself, to like anything about oneself is one of the greatest imaginable sins ... identical with selfishness or false pride*. Again, nothing could be further from the truth! Think of this: imagine you have a small child. Imagine you determine to make that child a God-fearing, responsible, and hard-working adult, and you decide to do so by following the above tenets, by not being fond of that child, by not loving that child. Do you think that child would prosper? I don't mean that it would die, but I do mean that bits of it would shrivel up and die, or at least, disappear, *because that child would need to be loved*. And so do we all – we need to love *ourselves* in order to be healthy on all levels.

* Of course it is not the Bible that forbids love of the self, but *how* the Bible has been interpreted.

Fromm, whom I referred to above, also mentions Kant:

"According to Kant, it is a virtue to want the happiness of others, while to want one's own happiness is ethically "indifferent," since it is something which the nature of man is striving for and a natural striving cannot have positive ethical sense. [...] love for oneself, striving for one's own happiness, can never be a virtue. As an ethical principle, the striving for one's own happiness "is the most objectionable one, not merely because it is false,... but because the springs it provides for morality are such as rather undermine it and destroy its sublimity..."

Clearly, our socialization - generally well-intentioned - has drastically skewed our way of thinking and behaving with respect to how we consider the topic of self-love, and until we become aware of the impact this has had on us, our beliefs, our lives, our relationships, and all that we have done, and consequently the impact this has had on our psycho-emotional and spiritual health and well-being, nothing will change. Until we emerge from the muddied morass of this erroneous belief structure, we will not be able to help ourselves. The mere possibility of *believing* that we have the right to help ourselves in this regard may jumpstart the process of self-love.

External Emphasis

Many raised in our culture are desperately reaching towards fame - towards becoming a celebrity of sorts. Make your video go viral on YouTube and be an overnight global success. Self-publish your book and if it's about the right subject at the right time, again, you might be that next million copy bestseller. But it's not so much the Rafael Nadal's or the Alicia Keyes's of this world that seek such fame, because they have been working hard for years to rise to the top of their field, as those who have been raised - *by our culture* - to believe that it is mainly through fame that we are worth something, and who moreover seem to have grown into a sense of entitlement: *I have a right to this and I should be able to get it without working hard for it.* My argument here is not based so much on whether what people with such ambitions are really after is the financial ease, as the fact that they believe on some level that this will make them feel really good - in general and about themselves. And of course, if we look at Margaux Hemingway, Kurt Cobain, or Amy Winehouse, to name only a few of those who chose to take their own lives, in this regard, we know that in the end, they did not, indeed, feel that life was good, despite their celebrity status.

We have placed incredible emphasis on the external: on our youth, our looks, the size and shape of our bodies, the labels on our clothing, the schools and universities we go to, the cars we drive, the places we vacation at, the professions we go into, the size of our bank accounts and portfolios, the social scene within which we move, our homes as well as their physical location, our partners and their looks and 'value' according to this externally measured scale, and of course, how important we are.

Many of us sigh at the superficiality of this, and yet most of us pay lip service to it. How did it get that way? While I don't pretend to know the answer to that question, I *do* know that we have lost the connection to our inner Self (I address this in depth in my book *Rewiring the Soul*) and in that process, many of us have decided that the best way to love ourselves is to fit into the above slots as best and as well as we can. So we measure our self-love by how much we have and achieve. And of course, in some fashion, we never stop comparing ourselves and what we have to others, where we can never win. We'll never be the youngest, the slimmest, the richest, the most important, the most popular, the most successful, the most intelligent, or the most powerful, and so the part where we figure out how to love ourselves somehow gets lost in the shuffle.

> No matter what age you are, or what your circumstances might be, you are special, and you still have something unique to offer. Your life, because of who you are, has meaning.
> Barbara de Angelis

There is of course nothing wrong with having and achieving, but what weight are you placing on it in order to assess your value in your own eyes and hence how much you feel you are capable of loving or honoring or respecting yourself? For that matter, how much weight are you placing on what you have and what you achieve in order to determine - in your mind - the extent of your *intrinsic* value in the eyes of *others*, and hence how much they may honor or respect you and hence how much you can then honor yourself? Do you see where this is going? It's all externally-based;

none of it has anything to do with a self-generated mode of love for the self based on something that is not out there, but in here, inside of you.

Furthermore, you use your peers as a barometer, a benchmark, not only to compare yourself to, but also to establish your own value. If you don't attain that external gold standard you've selected, you have nothing to honor yourself for, nothing to love yourself for. And guess what? There will almost inevitably be someone who excels more than you do on one of those planes that you're using to measure your own worth, and so you fight a losing battle.

In a nutshell, that describes at least parts of a great many of us; perhaps the majority of us. And it's not because we're superficial and unthinking, or at least, that is only part of it. Because our society places such high value on external accomplishments, we lose sight of the fact that such a value placement rarely connects with the inner self.

Look at some of the tabloid press in your country. What or who is plastered all over the front page? Is it not a celebrity of some kind who has either just achieved something outstanding or lost something outstanding? (Note: this is *not* about the celebrity's achievement being good or bad; I'm not making a value judgment. What this *is* about, however, is the fact that we as a whole, place such value on the achievement that created the celebrity-hood of that person). Who are the majority of television talk show hosts discussing (other than those few die-hards who continue to offer real news and marvelous documentaries)? Isn't it the same kind of thing, albeit perhaps on other levels, but the gist of the program is to show us, the viewers, some element of the life of someone who has either just achieved something outstanding or lost something outstanding? (And I use the word *outstanding* in a way that perhaps does not conform to the conventional dictionary definition as much as to that which we, as a culture, now call outstanding - which may be quite different from the former). And why does the tabloid press do so well? Why do those talk shows generate such huge audiences? *Because that is where we are at.* We are judging our peers on the basis of what is being achieved or lost. And because we do it to them, *we do it to ourselves.* We've totally lost sight of the fact that we are so much more than what we do, earn, accumulate and look like to others. And so we have difficulty in understanding that we need to learn to love the self if we ever want to be at peace inside. Inner well-being, joy, peace, and harmony all begin with loving the self, and if loving the self depends on what I have out there, as opposed to what I am and have inside, then as said, I will fight a losing battle all my life.

Thoughtful and articulate individuals fall into this trap. It's not one that only collects the lowest common human denominator, in case you were thinking that. Look at academia. *Publish or perish* and therein lie many nights of tossing and turning in stress at the thought that a colleague just got offered tenure and you did not. Look at office politics in any mid-level corporation. Look at the arts, and not only at the actual art that is being produced now by some incredibly brilliant people, but look at the jockeying among buyers - many who remain anonymous - of works of art from the past, where the *honor* goes to the individual who purchased the most expensive Monet or Van Gogh. While I don't doubt that it may be marvelous to own such a painting and have it hanging on my very own wall in my very own home, I wonder whether its enjoyment and value are derived from the actual beauty of the painting, or whether at least a portion of the enjoyment comes from its price tag and how the world viewed this acquisition. The possibility of such skewed thinking truly surrounds us on all levels, and as said earlier, we have become so immured to it, that we no longer appear to know and understand what is natural.

Our Culture's Refusal to Honor the Inner Quest

How often do you hear a child coming forward in a *show-and-tell* at school, explaining how he has been trying to connect to his inner voice by listening to what his body is telling him when he looks at Johnny and gets a tummy ache? It almost sounds ridiculous, doesn't it? How often have you gone to work and heard a colleague recount the story of a weekend spent in contemplation or meditation? Or recount the story of a weekend spent practicing being less judgmental and critical? How often have you told another of how your intuition led you to a specific bookstore, and once in it, to a specific section, and then a specific shelf where you found a book that has made a great difference in your life? I'm not insisting that these things don't happen, but I do insist that they happen relatively rarely because our culture not only does not tend to honor the inner quest, but those who *do* honor it, often feel embarrassed or shy about referring to their own connection to it.

I've frequently found myself - over the course of the chapters of my considerable life - sitting at a dinner table and having once again said something that is greeted with slightly strained silence. I dared to speak of the inner world. I dared to speak of the Self in capital letters. Admittedly, I know this, and in fact often avoid this unless I am in *appropriate or receptive* company, but sometimes I forget because I become wrapped up in an explanation about something and go on a bit too far, and am then faced with said silence.

If it were only a question of boredom, I would perhaps not insist on telling you about this. Personally I am less than fascinated by the topic of some sports. Long conversations about classical music do not rivet me to the spot, rather, they first cause my eyes to glaze over, and then to droop, and most of us can think of one topic or another that simply doesn't do it for us. But this topic involving the inner world is different. These reactions I have observed are most definitely not a question of boredom, but one of embarrassment, discomfort, and even polite - and occasionally less than polite - censure of a topic that the person listening to you does not seem to want to grant the right to be discussed at a dinner party. Don't misunderstand my words for an angry rant. This is not about equality of rights of topics for a dinner party, but about the fact that our culture continues to pay scant attention to the inner quest - often finding it, as illustrated here - embarrassing, and yet it is without a shadow of a doubt the inner quest that leads us to the greatest rewards.

> Find the love you seek, by first finding the love within yourself.
> Learn to rest in that place within you that is your true home.
> Sri Ravi Shankar

Without love for the self, such a quest is rarely undertaken, and yet, when an individual of any age begins to understand that loving the self can make such an ongoing difference in the quality of his life, the quest almost always follows, and in many instances the process is nearly automatic. It may begin with an examination of the life already lived to that point, or with greater self-reflection, all of which indicate the heightened interest the person begins to become aware of for connecting with the self. Whether undertaken on his own, or with some kind of guide, this often creates a sense of excitement and awakening.

Our collective cultural history is replete with so many myths and fairy tales that speak of such a quest in symbolic language, and of course, the 'seeker' is always some kind of hero, although he or she may not be that at all when the adventure begins. But because he finds the jewel, or saves the kingdom, or rescues the maiden or encounters the grail, he ultimately becomes the hero, as we can become the hero of our own lives in undergoing this inner quest with all the hurdles and obstacles it implies, as we grow to love the self.

Do Parents & Schools Teach Us to Love the Self?

Imagine having a teacher who is excellent at history and geography, and who can talk to you about all manner of things involved in those subjects, but has no inkling about trigonometry and algebra. Or imagine a teacher who is able to help you learn how to speak excellent French, but knows nothing of English literature. Clearly, such teachers would be tremendously lacking if we hoped to gain knowledge from them about the subjects in which they are not well-versed. We'd be considered fools if we were to seek them out for that.

How many of us, not to mention our children, have gone through the hands of teachers (and I would warrant that most of them are well-meaning and caring individuals) who simply know nothing about some of the most elementary and fundamental aspects of life, such as living consciously, being self-responsible, and loving the self? How *could* they know anything about these topics if they themselves were never taught how to do this? And were therefore also probably never taught how important to our well-being all of this is. Nevertheless, it is into these hands that we were placed as young, impressionable children, and it is into hands such as these that we place our own small and impressionable children. As far as I know, teachers are not even tested for something as (by now) normal as emotional intelligence, let alone, of course, the topic of this book, which is self-love. How could they be tested on this, if so few - and particularly not our educational institutions - are placing any kind of value on this?

And yet, that is where much of our early socialization takes place. I wish I could say that my files are filled with exceptions to this rule; that I have had numerous clients attest to being educated by individuals who placed importance on such topics and modeled these behaviors in ways that students were then able to internalize such teaching and manifest it in their own lives, but that is simply not the case. Quite the contrary - clients who are students now, i.e., teens, as well as clients who were students decades ago, recount the opposite of this, and naturally, therefore, are able to clearly state that the last thing they ever learned at school was a measure of self-love.

But of course, we simply cannot blame the teachers (or other caretakers) of our children for what we ourselves - as parents - are incapable of doing well. If we have not learned to love the self, our interaction with our children may be loving and caring, but it will always be missing one of the most important ingredients, which has much more to do with us, than with our children, and yet affects them so enormously, as we were similarly affected by our own unwitting parents.

Not loving the self may leave its cruel and often nearly indelible mark on our children in a myriad number of ways. Think of the mother who has never accessed her own childhood pain. Doesn't it make sense that one of the things she will never be able to teach her children is to examine the self in that self-reflective way that Socrates refers to when he stated: *the unexamined life is not worth living*? How could she, if she has not accessed the hurt? She will not be able to teach them how to develop a relationship with their own emotions, simply because she does not know about such relationships because her own emotions were stunted when she was a little girl. And yet, if such a mother learns how to love the self, she will be able to interact on a much different and healthier level with her children.

Or think of the kind of father who is emotionally unavailable for his little girl, or the kind of mother likewise for her little boy. An element of coolness will be apparent in such a relationship; an element of something that the child may pick up as rejection or lack of approval, and this, in turn, will affect the entire life trajectory of that child, until (or unless) he figures it out on his own, or finds a good therapist, and begins his own process of loving the self in order to undo what was - unwittingly - done to him in childhood.

> Believing in our hearts that who we are is enough is the
> key to a more satisfying and balanced life.
> Ellen Sue Stern

There are many other examples we could discuss, but one final one I want to offer here is the parent who has high expectations of his children. In and of itself, this is not a negative thing at all. It becomes negative when the children realize that approval, regard, and ultimately the highest measure of love from that parent is dependent on measuring up to those expectations. This will only ever happen with a parent whose own self-love is not internal, but dependent on some kind of accomplishment or achievement. Such a parent will produce children who are in constant stress, who do not know how to feel good about themselves, and who may deal with this stress and lack of inner approval by finding unhealthy relationships or resorting to substances in order to still the growling in their gut and the pain in their heart.

Parents don't set out to 'do' these things to their children! Parents commit these acts of omission because they don't know any better, and please believe me that it has nothing to do with demographics. It's not a question of a better education or a higher social position. It has to do with what our society does not include in all that it holds out to us as being desirable. We are encouraged to acquire wealth, fame, position, but we are not encouraged to look into the self.

In *Rewiring the Soul*, I wrote the following about parents who are unable to model self-love:

> Much of what we learn when we are children comes from modeling our parents. Clearly, if they are unable to demonstrate healthy love for the self in their own lives, we will not come to the conclusion that this is something we want for ourselves, because we simply won't be aware of it. They may be emotionally unavailable, needy, manipulative, controlling, rigid, or be perfectionists, have poor boundaries, obsessive thoughts or painful emotions. Please note that this is not about parent-bashing! Who can know how they, in turn, were raised by their own parents, and so on. This is simply about gaining perspective. No aspect of this type of behavior shows the child of such a parent how to love the self.
>
> We may grow into sophisticated and well-educated adults, with prestigious professions and glamorous social lives and may still not realize that we don't love ourselves. There may be an unidentified nagging of some kind deep inside on certain occasions, but it may take a difficult life transition or crisis - especially in our relationships - before we even come to understand that we are lacking this essential, nurturing and life-giving manner of caring for ourselves.

To learn this lesson is paramount, but not all learn it. Many may know in some deep, forgotten recess of their mind that their parents left much to be desired; many may resent that; many others may consciously be compassionate and forgive that, but only some learn that in order to fully move on in a healthy way, *parenting the self* has to occur - and that only happens if you embark on the road to loving the self.

> Knowing others is intelligence; knowing yourself is true wisdom.
> Mastering others is strength; mastering yourself is true power.
> If you realize that you have enough, you are truly rich.
> Lao Tzu

Chapter 4

Fearing the Self

People are like stained-glass windows. They sparkle and shine when the sun is out, but when the darkness sets in their true beauty is revealed only if there is light from within.
Elisabeth Kübler-Ross

How can you find your inner light if you fear the self? How can you find it if you don't know that one of the most wonderful things you can do in this life is to become connected and acquainted with the self? And how can you possibly find that inner light if you don't know *how* to connect to the self? Why do some people fear the self? What is there to fear? Where have they learned to fear the self?

The simple answer is that we tend to fear what we do not know. Didn't medieval mariners fear going out to sea due to the dragons they believed existed there? Perhaps some believed those dragons existed there because those who *had* gone out to sea had not returned. Others feared the sea because they believed the world was flat and that meant that they would fall off the edge to their death. They did not know this with certainty, but they feared it, and part of the fear came about due to the uncertainty. Rumors abounded about other lands with gold and glorious riches to be had for the taking, but few had ever met anyone who had, in fact, been in one of those lands, and so the whole thing was shrouded in fable, myth, and mystery.

The discovery of the New World in the 15th century is an ironic analogy to something that has been happening with more and more frequency and interest since the 1970's, although this other search is something that has been around for as long as man has existed. I'm referring to the interest in the life that may lie *beyond* life; what we might call the next and ultimate frontier. What happens when we die, and, if reincarnation does, in fact, exist, what exactly happens in those in-between life states? Where is the one who died while he/she 'waits' to be reborn? Who decides whether and when you will return, and for that matter how, under what circumstances and with which gender, race, and socio-economic conditions? How are the members of your family decided upon, as well as partners and relationships you may have during the next life? (My upcoming book, *The Master Calls A Butterfly*, deals with this topic extensively). You may feel that you have become uncomfortable as you just read this. Perhaps these are subjects you prefer not to entertain, because you do not believe in their veracity, or perhaps they make you afraid. Either way, for the mariners who feared going far out to sea, or the modern-day explorers who delve into the realms of the after-life and between-life state, fear tends to accompany the unknown - *except for those few who only experience an inner sense of excitement and exhilaration when they contemplate the next great adventure* and thus are able to lead the way for the rest.

Back to the self. What many fear is what they do not know. Think: when have you been encouraged to get to know yourself? In all likelihood you've learned inter-personal skills since you first went to pre-school or kindergarten, but when did anyone sit you down and mention that you also need to work on getting to know yourself and on treating yourself well? Parents and educators are becoming more savvy about this and conditions are certainly changing to some degree, but if you are not a child, the probability of you having been given an education where self-knowledge and self-love formed part of the agenda, is slight to null.

This Unknown Stranger (*Stranger From a Strange Land*)

Clearly, then, the self is a stranger. We often know our friends and colleagues better than ourselves. We may be able to offer them excellent advice that we would never properly figure out how to give ourselves, either because we would not listen to it, or because we would not consider we need it because our self-knowledge is too limited.

It's fundamental to begin something - anything - to correct that limitation and to begin to have an inkling of who you are. Here are some relatively simple things you can begin to do immediately, and until you start seeing the treasure you are about to unveil, and will *crave* doing this, you need not even spend a great deal of time on it. Remember that knowing the self is - in part - *reflecting* upon the self, and self-reflection implies reflecting upon one's life. It was Socrates who said: *the unexamined life is not worth living*, and it was Aristotle who said: *knowing yourself is the beginning of all wisdom*. If you set out to follow all or at least some of the following suggestions, your life will become enormously enriched; if you let it go, or decide to do it at some other time, you will not have access to the treasure inside. It was Jung who said: *your vision will become clear only when you look into your heart. Who looks outside, dreams. Who looks inside, awakens.*

Examine your time line: This often results in being one of the most interesting self-reflective exercises you can do. Take one piece of paper for each year of your life. If you are 52, you will need 52 sheets of paper. At the top of each sheet, write your age (0 years, 1 year, 2 years, etc.), and the year in question, i.e., in 1981 you were five. Then write down the address (if you don't remember the street, just put the city or the subdivision of the city in which you lived each year), as well as who lived with you at that location that year, i.e., your parents, your paternal grandmother, your older siblings, the dog. Also write down the kindergarten, school, or college you were attending, or the company at which you were working. Make a note of important friends, neighbors, or colleagues. This entire preamble serves to jog your memory about that year of your life. If you will leave the sheaf of papers lying in a convenient location, perhaps on your bedroom dresser, each time you think of something, you can add it to the appropriate year. It may take you a while to 'populate' the sheets, but you will begin to see pieces of a puzzle emerging, and you will begin to understand yourself better. You may also begin to see aspects of yourself that you had never considered. (See Appendix C for a Sample)

Keep a journal: There are no rules to this journal writing exercise. Write whatever you wish. Perhaps you start by writing about going to get your hair cut, but as you continue, you remember the conversation you had with someone there while you waited, and how that conversation brought back a memory of your father and that put you into a pensive state because of the last words you said to each other before he died some years ago. Or perhaps you start by writing about how annoyed you are with your partner for his/her refusal to discuss certain issues you feel are of paramount importance, and that takes you to another conversation you had in which it was your *partner* who was saying the same thing to you, about your *own* refusal to participate in conversations about sex. Or perhaps you start by writing about the glory of your garden that you can see from the window where you sit as you write, and that's it - you simply describe your garden. However it comes out, and however you express yourself, it is a mechanism whereby you are coming closer to yourself - to your Self, and this process can offer you magnificent gifts. There are journals, personal correspondence, and autobiographies by others that may fascinate, stimulate, or enthrall you, such as those by Thoreau, Simone de Beauvoir, Ken Wilber, Anäis Nin, Thomas Mann, Martin Luther King, Jean Houston, Nelson Mandela, Agatha Christie, or Carl Gustav Jung, to mention only a few. The possibilities and lists are endless and the potential inspiration is breath-taking. This will also help lead you closer to your Self.

> It is impossible for anyone to be responsible for another person's behavior. The most you or any leader can do is to encourage each one to be responsible for himself.
> Robert A. Heinlein

Keep a dream journal: Again, no rules, but try to make a habit of this, because otherwise, you will generally forget your dreams. If you wake up in the middle of the night remembering a dream, make sure you have some paper at your bedside, and if you don't sleep alone, you may wish to have a small flashlight on your night table as well, and record your dream by its light out of respect for your partner's sleep. If you wake up in the morning and remember a dream, *try not to move* prior to going through the dream at least once in chronological order, as best as you recall it, and then reversing the order until you get back to the beginning. This helps 'fix' the dream in your memory, because it is a well-known fact by dream researchers that if you move before doing an exercise similar to the one just described, you tend to forget most of the dream, despite having a clear picture of it in your mind before the movement. At any rate, record the dream, noting date and time if appropriate, you might also wish to note a few bullet points about anything that has taken place in the last 24 hours (whether you think it has a bearing on the dream or not), because when you go back to interpret the dream later, or when you re-read the dream even years later, those bullet points may be of great use to you in understanding. Clearly, if you wish to interpret the dream, you'll have to read at least a book or two about dreams, and there are many noted in the Bibliography. The Talmud says: *A dream not interpreted is like a letter not read*, and I tend to agree with that. In some fashion a part of you is trying to communicate with another part of you. If you simply pay no attention to your dreams, or make no attempt to understand what they may be telling you, then you are wasting a highly valuable resource *intrinsic* to your own being that will also - as all the others we are discussing in this section - bring you closer into relationship with your Self.

Examine your relationships, including your friendships: If you have already read another one of my books *The Tao of Spiritual Partnership*, you will be familiar with the relationship patterns described in it. However, even if you have not read it, you can begin to analyze your love relationships first (because they tend to be slightly more dramatic in our memory than most of our friendships), on the basis of *what* you fell in love with (characteristics, please, not physical aspects, prowess, or beauty) in the other person, and what then created the beginning of the demise and the actual end of the relationship (if it has ended). As you look over even those early teenage romances, and compare them on the basis of the above questions, you can place them under the lens of your microscope and you may find that you begin to discern patterns. Were there similar roadblocks in more than one of your relationships? Did you trip over the same crack more than once? Were you blind at the beginning to similar aspects across more than one relationship that then became brilliantly clear to you in the aftermath? If you mainly see patterns (that you began to realize in the course of the relationship) about what was wrong with the *other* party, you may wish to examine yourself in the light of being the person who *chose* that other party, and try to discover the reason for such a choice of such a (supposedly) *wrong* partner. Could there have been deeper and hidden (to you) motives for this? Could your psyche or your soul have moved you towards a relationship with that *so-called wrong* partner precisely in order to learn something and then to grow thanks to that? This is a somewhat psycho-spiritual route to follow in finding a connection to the Self, but it can be of great value if you give it profound consideration. Follow a similar process with your friendships, although you may find that in the majority of those, there is no demise, at least not such a clearly defined one as in the love relationships.

Mindfulness: This book cannot possibly hope to do justice to a topic that has been covered in numerous outstanding volumes (some are in the Bibliography), in just a few words. However, there is one excellent definition for mindfulness offered by Jon Kabat-Zinn, considered by some the Western father of the subject (after learning about it from Thich Nhat Hanh during a retreat), and that definition is this: *paying attention in a particular way: on purpose, in the present moment, and non-judgmentally*. What happens when you practice this? You begin to quiet the mind. You begin to become aware of yourself and your surroundings in a way that you are not able to as long as your mind is not quiet and is dominated by your irrepressible thoughts that arise continually and not of your own volition.

In order to come to such a place; in order to be able to accomplish this, you need to have a mindfulness practice (also see Appendix B). There are many ways of going about this, but one, very simple one, is this: Consider taking a brief, 15-minute walk every day, a relaxing walk, not one in which you can't catch your breath. Do it alone, without another person and also without a pet. The main focus in this walk is to become aware of your present surroundings by using the beauty of what there is. Simply focus on the first beautiful thing you see or hear - perhaps an oak tree that has just begun to show its first green buds in the spring, or the song of robins. As you look at or listen to whatever it is you have chosen, feel grateful for that presence in your life just now, and notice a light sensation of relaxation or peace in your solar plexus. Now notice the next thing. Perhaps you now see a crocus bursting through the ground or you hear the sound of wind through the trees. Again, notice the beauty, feel the gratitude, and notice the sensation of peace. Now perhaps you see a kitten trying to catch a fly or you hear the contagious laughter of a child, or you smell the heady perfume of a night jasmine. Remember to notice the beauty, feel the gratitude, and then notice the sensation of peace. And this time perhaps you see a trail of busy worker ants carrying tiny bits of a plant into their underground colony, or you hear the sound of cicadas. As before, notice the beauty, feel the gratitude, and notice the sensation of peace. Simply continue to do this for 15 minutes until you come to the end of your walk.

The reason you feel a sensation of peace, even though it may only last a few moments, is because you are no longer in the pain or suffering of your past (in your thoughts), nor are you in the stress and worry of your future (in your thoughts). You have left both of those *non-now moments* in order to access the present; the *now*, by focusing on beauty and gratitude. The more you do this, the greater amount of time you will find yourself spending in the present, and the more your inner peace will take up permanent residence in your being.

However, here's what will happen, at least at the beginning. You will probably feel temporarily cheerful during those first few moments of awareness as you take in beauty and notice peace. However, in all likelihood you will very quickly forget the intended purpose of your walk and will go into a relatively *unaware* world of thoughts and hence back to stress. And only when you realize that your fifteen minutes are up, will you remember what you were supposed to be doing.

Don't worry. If you do this every day for about three weeks, your neural pathways will begin to change such that you will realize that you are closer and closer to managing the 15 minutes of noticing beauty and feeling appreciation and gratitude, and hence feeling more relaxed and at peace. This will impact all areas of your life, and each time you do it will bring you into greater *connection* with your Self. It will also radically change your neural pathways. It's so simple. All you need to do is do it and then continue doing it.

Read: Read books by great philosophers, thinkers, or spiritual masters that resonate with you. By finding that resonance with wisdom that others have written about - even if they did so many centuries ago - you connect to your Self. The reason you resonate is because somewhere in you there is a part that *knows* what you are resonating with; that already knew it, but had not, perhaps, remembered it yet. And so you discover more and more of your forgotten fragments. If you are at a loss as to where exactly to begin, browse through the Bibliography of this book. When you find something that sounds interesting, Google it on Amazon in order to read a further description of the book. Read some of the reviews. You will know whether or not it is a book that you would benefit by reading.

Collect: Begin to collect quotations, passages from books that mean something to you, and audio and/or video clips that inspire, motivate, and move you. Upon examination, you will further discover aspects of the Self that only emerge because you are seeing them (aspects of the Self) through these selections you have made. They are part of you, and this helps you 'discover' yourself in yet another way. Also, such a collection will stand you in good stead when you need something to pick up your energy. I've been doing it since I was in my early teens. (Also see a sample list in Appendix D).

Life Cycles: Examine your life cycles. You might start by choosing some of the most salient moments in your life. Perhaps the most difficult. Or the most joyous. Write down the general time period in your life when they took place. More often than not, such cycles move over a period of months, not just one day. So perhaps you lost your job and found a new one over a period of nine months. Or perhaps a relationship broke up over a period of two years. At any rate, once you have those most important ones listed, go back seven years prior to the time of any of those events, or seven years forward, and see what, if anything, happened then. You may find a correlated event; an event that somehow connects with the earlier or later one, but especially if it is a later one, you may see how you have progressed in that one, as opposed to the earlier one, in the manner in which you dealt with it, understood it, grew from it, etc.

Doing such exercises also connect you more closely to your Self, as you begin to see more and more pieces of the puzzle of your life coming together. (Note: for those of you familiar with humanistic astrology, this relates to the cycles of Saturn over the course of an entire life trajectory. Examining your life to the point you currently find yourself at on this basis can be highly illuminating).

> When you are content to be simply yourself and don't compare or compete, everyone will respect you.
> Lao Tzu

Meditate: If you wish to use the tool of meditation to find the road to the Self, and if you have not already learned how to meditate, you may prefer to take a course, or to read another book solely dedicated to that practice. However, simply said, by sitting comfortably in a quiet place where you will not be disturbed for the period of time you wish to meditate, by then closing your eyes and following your breath, perhaps repeating either a mantra, or the syllable OM, or any other words or sounds you may find beneficial for this practice, you will, without needing to take a course, be able to meditate. Continue bringing your attention back to your breath, the mantra, or the syllable, each time you find your mind wandering. Start with a short period of time (five minutes, for example), and build your way up to longer periods.

Spiritual path: Some people find it more comfortable to follow an already existing spiritual path as they go down that growth-inducing road that leads them closer to the Self. While I personally find this less than satisfactory, I do recognize that for some it is very beneficial, and so it may be a way you wish to pursue. Perhaps you have read of the teachings of a specific person or feel drawn to a particular religion that speaks to you and therefore you want to move in that direction. This way is as valid as every other way, because in the end, all roads truly do lead to Rome - to that same place where we connect with the Self in a way that allows us to love the self.

****

Remember, all of these suggestions are merely guidelines to help you make your way up a scaffolding of sorts that is holding your essence together. How this scaffolding then becomes an actual building of beauty, will depend on how much time you spend in this process, how much you decide to allow it to give to you, and whether you are even interested in making something of the bare bones that are visible via the scaffolding. Connecting with and coming to know the Self is a process of much work, but also much discovery and beauty. Your rewards will be endless.

The Terror of Being Vulnerable

Horror movies or frightening situations in crime thrillers make the idea of being vulnerable to attack very visceral. As you watch such scenes on the screen at the cinema or in your home on television, you can feel your heart pounding, and you might even look away in order to avoid seeing the part that you know is about to occur. You may number among the many people who feel a little like this when they think of opening up to someone emotionally; of baring their inner self, their private thoughts and fears to a partner or potential partner, who - although that person professes to love you - may, at some point, stop doing so, or simply betray you, and may then make use of this intimate information gleaned from you when you offered yourself up in this vulnerable way and thus harm you emotionally.

And therein lies the reason why there are so many individuals who simply never really open up to another. These are the ones we might call emotionally unavailable. We have already seen that we could define these individuals as those who fear their own emotions because deeply-felt emotions open the door to vulnerability. Therefore emotionally unavailable people have little contact with their own emotions and they certainly experience some difficulty empathizing with the emotions of others.

> She lacks confidence, she craves admiration insatiably. She lives on the reflections of herself in the eyes of others. She does not dare to be herself.
> Anäis Nin

Another group of people that *stops* opening up to others is the one that has been burned in a prior relationship. These individuals fell in love, they opened up to great vulnerability and they were betrayed (or believe they were betrayed) in some fashion. So they decided they would never do that again, thank you very much. Falling in love is a much too dangerous venture for them to consider embarking upon ever again. They freeze emotionally in some fashion in order to prevent any future hurt. The fact that they therefore condemn themselves to an emotionally barren life, is not something they tend to recognize at the point at which they make such a decision; in fact, they may not realize that this is what they have done, until much later, perhaps in the last decade or two of life, as they realize how frozen and stagnant their emotions have become, even if they have continued to engage in relationships.

And of course there are numerous other sub-sets of people who may not be so easily labeled as I've done here, but who nevertheless due to childhood situations or other issues later on in life, and particularly in their relationships, have closed up lock, stock, and barrel, and do not open up to whatever might make them feel vulnerable to hurt again.

This terror of vulnerability is, of course, dreadful. It's awful for a burgeoning relationship, but perhaps even more insidious for you if you have taken such a decision for your life - possibly for the remainder of your days, despite still being perhaps reasonably young. The reason for this is connected to the fact that it signifies that you may never be able to truly connect to the self. Not allowing vulnerability means that an entire sector of the self and the Self is totally closed off from you, as well as from any potential partner. (If you have not already read the difference between *Self* and *self* as I use it in the book, please see Appendix E).

It was Jung who said that we most come to know ourselves through our relationships with others, and if those relationships remain emotionally barren, the road into the Self remains impassable. Our relationships with others - especially our love relationships - show us many aspects of the self by virtue of the mirror of our reactions to the other. An example of this would be any emotion that arises in you as you interact with your partner. Even if you feel that your partner has provoked - and perhaps even *deliberately* provoked - this reaction, it is *your* reaction that can tell you something about yourself. It could be that you need to investigate your boundaries with regards to this recurring behavior on the part of your partner and erect healthier boundaries in order to stop this from happening (or decide on other possible outcomes, should your partner be unwilling to participate in the conversation), or - and this is just as often the case as the other possibility - you might need to look more closely at yourself by virtue of your reaction in order to better understand why you have such a strong reaction about something that is, in fact, something relatively small. Either way, it is *your* reaction to your partner, i.e., what you see in that mirror of your relationship with your partner, that shows you something about the self.

How can this possibly happen if you don't engage emotionally because you are afraid of being vulnerable? The passage into the Self comes - at least in part - through opening up to another.

The Dread of Rejection

The fear of rejection is in some sense a kissing cousin of the fear of vulnerability. As discussed, being rejected hits you in a very painful place indeed. It hits you in your self-esteem, and of course if your self-esteem is dependent on outer factors, *you may find it hard to recuperate from rejection.*

We've all been there - we asked someone for something - a date, a job, a raise, a loan, help in doing something, forgiveness, love, a recommendation, and so on, and we were rejected. Or we started up a business - like a restaurant - but then not enough clients came and so we felt rejected. Oh the devastation inside! The feeling of utter failure and yes, rejection.

As touched on earlier, rejection gives rise to many feelings that make us doubt our own self-worth, that cause us to put great big question marks around our value as men, women, human beings. The fact that we have been rejected makes many other accomplishments we may have under our belt pale in comparison. We arbitrarily give the rejection tremendous power over our own judgment of ourselves.

Inherent in this lies not only our sense of self esteem, self acceptance, and self love, but more importantly, our sense of self confidence, or to put it in more exact terms, our sense of inner security about ourselves.

In other words, if we have a strong sense of inner security, and if we believe – with all our being – in the essence of our value as a human being, as a man, or a woman, then rejection will merely appear to be a mild ripple in a pond on a warm summer day. If, however, our sense of inner security depends on validation from sources external to ourselves, then rejection may appear to be as overwhelming as a Category 5 hurricane, and in its devastating and annihilating power, sweep us off our feet, robbing us of initiative and pro-activity.

> If you believe that feeling bad or worrying long enough will change a past or future event, then you are residing on another planet with a different reality system.
> William James

This is the insidious power of rejection to paralyze us. We fear what we call failure, and failure is implicit in rejection for those who identify their self-worth and inner security with external approbation and acceptance. And yet, remember what you may have read on numerous occasions: how often was Abraham Lincoln rejected by the electorate, for Congress, for the Senate, and ultimately for the Presidency, before he was finally elected? Did this stop him from trying again? How often did Edison's attempts at inventing a usable light bulb end in failure? Did this stop him from trying again? Beethoven was considered hopeless at composing by his music teacher - evidently this did not stop him from doing precisely that. The New York Times pronounced the idea of television as something the average family would never want in their homes, and Warner Brothers said talking movies would never be a success, and yet clearly this did not stop all those who were promoting these ideas.

We must be aware of the power of rejection, and therefore take preventive measures in order that when we meet up with it, it does not take the rhythm out of our lives. Clearly, no one is entirely impervious to rejection, and no one can totally ignore it. Indeed, on occasion rejection may indicate that steps must be taken in order to improve on something that is not giving the desired results. A scriptwriter, for example, faced with numerous rejections from directors, may consider some of their suggestions for improving the manuscript. An actor who is rejected after each audition, may consider taking some additional acting classes. A politician who is rejected in each election, may consider carefully examining the position he or she takes on specific issues.

However, and this is very important, even if the rejection causes a person to try to improve something, the fact of the matter is, that the worth and value of that person are no different before and after upgrading their chosen activity. And it is precisely this which people with a negligible sense of inner security do not see. Therefore it behooves every individual to work on building up and expanding this sense of inner security.

This means self-awareness has to become the name of the daily game. In particular, your own self-talk must be closely observed. What are you telling yourself? How are you reacting in given situations? What are your feelings about the events that occur? Once you begin to glimpse what kind of dialogue goes on inside of you at least for a portion of the time (because to become conscious of all of this all of the time, takes a while, and a bit of discipline), then you can ascertain where your inner security needs some tweaking.

Try to see a pattern in your self-talk, your reactions, and feelings. Remember to also take stock of your physical reactions at each of these steps - is your breathing suddenly more shallow or is your solar plexus twisting in pain, or is there perhaps an unexpected lump in your throat? Become conscious not only of the pattern of your thoughts, self talk, reactions, and feelings, but also of the pattern of your body's reactions.

> Scarcity of self value cannot be remedied by money, recognition, affection, attention or influence.
> Gary Zukav

More than likely the pattern will be dancing around the issue of how you tend to make mistakes, or how you are supposed to be perfect, or how dumb you are, or how you can never get it right, or how people just don't seem to like you, or another variation on this same theme. Seeing the pattern will help you counteract it, because on those occasions where you actually catch yourself "in the pattern", once you have established what it is, you will be able to bring consciousness or awareness, rather than blindness, into the reaction. So you will be able to turn the thought, or the reaction, or the feeling into something more positive, more self-affirming, something that, in other words, works affirmatively on your sense of inner security. Once you have begun this process, observe how you begin to feel differently when you get a new rejection.

More than anything, of course, is the underlying fact that once you have learned to love the self, fear of rejection, just like fear of vulnerability, will begin to fade. As long as your sense of self-esteem and inner security comes from within as opposed to from without, none of these fears will ever have any power over you again.

Facing the Truth (The Shadow)

A simplistic quest for happiness that does *not* involve approaching the darker sides of one's psyche with care and awareness, is one that is bound to fail to some degree, if not entirely. You can only keep up appearances for a while, if you don't bother trying to understand where your darkness lies. I referred earlier to medieval alchemists and their quest to transform coal into gold, offering the analogy of the darkness of the human shadow that we attempt to transform into light in this process of finding and loving the Self.

I lean towards much of Jung's work, as well as that of the neo-Jungians, as I do towards many Buddhist teachings, and so I do believe that it is necessary to have such a *confrontation* with your own darkness if you truly wish to find a path to inner peace. In other words, to glibly proclaim that by thinking positively you will find deep and lasting happiness is, of course, a denial of the depth of the psyche and all that lies therein. Without an acquaintance and close understanding of that part of you, peace will not come.

> Until you make the unconscious conscious, it will direct
> your life and you will call it fate.
> Carl Gustav Jung

However, having said that, I fully support living positively *no matter what your circumstances.* I take courage from the example of lives such as Mandela, Frankl, Christopher Reeve and many others who demonstrated that living positively in the light of horrific personal circumstances *made all the difference in their lives and the quality of their lives during those trying circumstances.*

Living positively as a part of our daily routine means that on some level we *choose* to look at things, whatever they may be from the position of *possibility* rather than from one of *desperation*. This - believing in possibility - is in and of itself, already a measure of potentially greater well-being (akin to happiness), than focusing on *what is wrong.* If we set our focus on the shadow and the darkness within, we may lose *sight* of what is *possible.* Therein lies, I believe the greatest strength and value of positive psychology: it has allowed us to see the merit of *choosing where to focus our eyes,* followed by choosing where to focus our *thoughts,* followed therefore, by choosing where to focus our *feelings.*

This is not a subject to be bantered about blithely, but it *is* a subject where the positivists need some defending - even by one who strongly believes in the importance of examining the dark.

> A man who as a physical being is always turned towards the outside, thinking that his happiness lies outside him, finally turns inward and discovers that the source is within him.
> Sören Kierkegaard

Some thoughts about happiness and enlightenment that you may find encouraging:
- Happiness: not minding what happens (Krishnamurti)
- Happiness: accepting what is (Eckhart Tolle)
- Enlightenment: the quiet acceptance of what is (Wayne Dyer)

Facing the shadow, which we might also describe as facing the truth about yourself, can be an exquisitely, albeit painfully, enriching process where what you learn about yourself both broadens you and liberates you. What happens to the darkness when you shine a light in it? It is dispelled and you can see, and if what you see are cobwebs or trash or discarded, broken items, clearly, due to the fact that you can now see, you are able to gather them, throw them out, sweep and in general, make of that place that is now so beautifully lit, a clean and welcoming place. None of that was possible when it was still dark, other than by stumbling over the rubbish and broken items, possibly even hurting yourself, or walking into the cobwebs and startling yourself, at the very least.

If you have been diligent and have practiced at least some of the activities suggested earlier in this chapter, you will have noticed that you have been shining light on your inner self, that aspects of yourself and your Self have come into consciousness (another way of referring to light), and that you have begun to know yourself in ways you did not before. This is part of the process of loving the self; this intimate meeting with the Self by the process of self-examination and self-reflection allows you to move into deep connection with the Self and therein lies a love and sensation of inner peace and freedom that you have probably never known before. Bringing the shadow - the truth about yourself - into the light is no mean feat and worthy of comparison with the mystic quest for the grail. The treasure within is the greatest treasure of all.

Once that treasure becomes clearly visible to you, and once you begin to partake of all its blessings, knowing, and depth, your life will have changed forever. *Nothing can be compared to this.* Think of the life of a beggar who was always cold and hungry, and then contrast it to his life the day he is taken in by a compassionate, kind, and generous patron. Before he had nothing, now he has all he could ever need. In our analogy, before you are able to see the treasure within - the Source that is You - you are never at peace, you are always insecure, or stressed, or afraid, or worried, or any other kind of negative emotion you care to mention. In order to *not* feel that way, you require external elements to be in place, and they only work for a time. Once the treasure becomes evident to you, you no longer need anything outside yourself - outside your Self - to keep you safe, loved, and cared for, because all of this now lies within your hands; you have become that loving, benevolent, kind, compassionate and generous patron of yourself. Does this not remind you of the many times you have heard the parable of the man who went seeking riches, and left his home and sought high and low, in distant countries, and yet, when he finally returned, to the place from which he had initially started, he discovers that the riches had been there all along?

> We shall not cease from exploration
> And the end of all our exploring
> Will be to arrive where we started
> And know the place for the first time
> T.S. Eliot

Chapter 5

Seeking Love Everywhere but in the Self: Avoiding the Self

Everything in the universe is within you. Ask all from yourself.
Rumi

Have you ever procrastinated about meeting a deadline of some kind? You keep putting it off, you keep avoiding doing whatever it is that you should be doing, and if you continue in that vein, and if it's something that is expected of you in your profession, and if you avoid enough important deadlines, then you may soon find yourself without a job. However, when you avoid the Self, you don't get a pink slip or a letter of termination, but you create a greater and greater distance and lack of direct knowledge between yourself, your daily life, and the Self.

You tend to avoid the Self - which is the most exquisite and perfect place to find love for yourself - by looking for love elsewhere. There are many mechanisms for doing this and in this chapter we will examine some of the most common.

Food, Alcohol, Substances & Other Addictions

This one is simple to understand, and perhaps one of the most frequent and hence abused ways of avoiding the Self. It's also the one that at first glance *appears* to offer most comfort, succor, and solace, but of course, what it offers in fact, is nothing like comfort, succor, and solace, but addiction. You feel bad about yourself or about something that is happening in your life (it may be as simple as being *bored*, or as far-reaching as fearing the loss of your job, home, health, or love partner), and you reach for your substance of choice. It alleviates some of the problem, at least for a period of time. Whether you eat to do this, or control what you eat to do this, or whether you exercise too many hours a day, or drink in excess, or take drugs, or gamble, or shop until you drop, or indulge in risky sex, whichever your choice is, you crave it, because for a period of time you feel better.

I was a heavy smoker until 1988, smoking about four packs a day in the last few years, and when I finally stopped, I did so from one day to the next, and consider myself fortunate and blessed to have had an easy transition. Never once have I wanted to go back, not even for one lungful of smoke. Quite the contrary, I want nothing to do with cigarettes, although being around smokers does not particularly bother me, unless I'm surrounded on all sides. But here's the thing: when I stopped, of my own volition, and without a health scare, I did so mainly because I was absolutely incensed with myself for being controlled by this substance, apart from the fact that I assumed it would sooner or later oblige me to pay a price that involved my health. What I did not expect, was my nearly uncontrollable anger in certain situations after I stopped smoking.

Whenever I was provoked in ways that before would not have unduly bothered me (someone taking my parking spot, for instance), I became ferociously and outrageously angry. I couldn't recognize myself and quickly realized that the cigarettes had kept a lid on my anger, although I had not been aware of it over the two decades that I smoked. So the moral of the tale is that in my case, this particular substance kept a rather volatile emotion in a place where I did not have to deal with it. Once I had stopped and recognized this, obviously I *did* have to deal with it. Discussing this one day with a friend, she confessed that when *she* had stopped smoking, she became depressed and that only when she began to smoke again, did the depression lift. I ventured the opinion that the smoking might have been keeping a lid on her depression similar to what occurred in my case with the anger, but she would have needed to stop smoking again to discover whether it truly was the case and to then work on her depression, and it became obvious to me that she did not want to.

> Your problem is you're too busy holding onto your unworthiness.
> Ram Dass

I had no difficulty in understanding her - she had grown accustomed to her 'easy' fixes for the feelings that pressed on her, and in particular, bearing in mind much of it was unconscious, just as in my case I had not been aware of cigarettes having a hand in tamping down my anger, it made sense to me that she preferred to have a quick fix, as opposed to having to learn how to cope on her own. But of course this is all wrong. Our connection to the self, our love for the self should be capable of so much more, and it is heartbreaking to see in so many instances all over our global community, the hell into which people have brought themselves, all because our culture places such little importance on knowing and loving the self.

Think about how many people have to deal with eating disorders because it is via food that they are able to avoid going into the self in order to discover what it is that is causing them to feel the way they do, feelings they wish to escape from that stop them from feeling good. Eating provides comfort, which is why we call many foods - even for those who don't have eating disorders - *comfort* foods. Exactly the same assumptions could be made about the behavior of those who drink to excess or those who use drugs: recreational or prescription. (Note: while the demonstrated chemically addictive nature of most processed foods also plays a role, that topic is outside the scope of this book).

What then often occurs is this process of avoiding I've referred to several times, but it generally begins blindly; i.e., the person using the substance or food is unaware of the fact that by so doing a potentially life-long, dangerous, health- and happiness-destroying process of avoiding some difficult feeling is being brought into existence. It might begin simply because a young teen is offered a few beers by an older friend at a party. He gets a buzz and likes the fact that the buzz makes him feel less tense, or allows him to focus on something different than his anger. Or perhaps he is offered a joint and soon feels relaxed. The problem is not so much the actual substance, as the fact that the young person notices a lessening of the difficult emotion and now connects the substance with that lessening and begins to regard the substance as his/her friend.

Just for a moment imagine a world of aware individuals. They would have learned at home and in school at a very young age to discern and recognize their own emotions and to deal with them in healthy ways. They would have learned to love the self and self-soothe and take responsibility for the self and the combination of all of this - none of which is very hard to take on board, especially if it happens early on in life - simply means that because they are already taking care of their emotions, while they may enjoy a substance of some kind, I posit that they would rarely seek it out to avoid confronting difficult emotions and to avoid the self. They would not need to. They would already feel good enough *without* need for any kind of substance. What a world that would be!

We are not taught to self-soothe (for much more on this topic, see *Rewiring the Soul*), we are also not taught to be self-reflective (if we *were*, we would not be avoiding the self, as being self-reflective already implies connecting to the self), nor to recognize the point at which we need to take charge of our inner well-being in such a way that we can - at the very least - regain a measure of inner equilibrium.

Drama & Need

Most of us have met at least one so-called 'drama queen/king' in our lives, and we understand that this type of person somehow requires drama to keep his life moving forward, as unhealthy as all that drama may be. *'You'll never guess what happened to me today'*, John may tell us when we meet for coffee, or Suzanne informs us that *'Mark'* (her ex-partner) *'picked up the kids from school today without even letting me know, so I've had to see my lawyer'.* They thrive on continual drama in some fashion, and it keeps their adrenaline going. It also keeps them from thinking, focusing, being present, self-reflecting, making good choices, and being aware, to name only a few. In other words, it helps them avoid the Self.

Clients often come in for the first session and begin to tell me their particular story - often a dreadfully triangulated and involved tale of passion, love, hate, victimhood, and pain. Since my goal is to offer clients some guidelines to follow right from the first session, I tend to intervene 20 minutes or so before the end, in order to be able to do this, and as I explain what - in my opinion - might help them move forward immediately to at least feel marginally better in their specific situation, I can see their eyes glazing over as they lean towards me, focused on my lips, to pounce in the slightest moment of silence in order to be able to continue with their own tale of woe.

Don't misunderstand: this is not a judgement or criticism of this behavior, but a pointing out of it in order that you may see the intense manner in which this individual is involved with the story of his own drama, frequently to the exclusion of a great deal of the rest of whatever is occurring in the present moment. These people are suffering so much and are so intent on their story that they find it difficult, if not impossible, to focus on anything else. If you are friends, they may continually interrupt when you are trying to offer help or advice, because they are simply not hearing you, or else they are only hearing the 'yes, but' part of their own answer, because for them their drama is so intense, that well-intentioned words rarely, if ever, reach fertile ground in their minds.

What is important to recognize here is the fact that such a person is *using* the drama and the intense involvement in it as a mechanism with which the Self can be avoided, much as an alcoholic will use alcohol, or an addict will use drugs. Remember that the encounter with the Self begins by facing your own demons, your own shadow, your own issues, and these avoidance mechanisms allow you to keep from doing precisely that. Is this being done consciously? More often than not, it is being done blindly. You can only avoid the Self consciously once you've understood much of what we are talking about here, and while the topic is most certainly not original to this book, it is, nevertheless, as we've seen, something which is not generally addressed in our culture and our educational system. Therefore, when we think about striving for something, it tends to consist of external benefits and not the quest that this undertaking requires. That's why mythology and fairy tales are so rich with metaphor in addressing this search and often call it the hero's journey, or the quest for the grail. What is heroic about it, is the fact that it's not easy at all, that it often involves going against the accepted norm and making yourself look different or strange, and it *always* involves overcoming many inner challenges in order to free the princess from the dragon or to find the magic potion that will save the king's life and rescue the kingdom. And of course the grail is often used as a symbol for divine grace, and it could be said that the search for the Self is a search for the divine within.

> A loving person lives in a loving world. A hostile person lives in a hostile world. Everyone you meet is your mirror.
> Ken Keyes

When drama is used as a way of avoiding the self, need is often also involved. This is an urgent need for another human being in such a way that if the other withdraws, the one who needs suffers from withdrawal symptoms that can be compared to withdrawal from a substance. The reason that this occurs is because the needy person's well-being is tied up with the love and availability of the other and this typically has its roots in early childhood where for some reason the child either did not learn to love itself or became overly dependent on one of the parents but in some way was not properly responded to.

Imagine, for example, a little girl whose father is not available for her. Perhaps he is never at home because he works too much, perhaps he is cold and rejecting or disapproving, perhaps he simply is not there at all, because he and the mother have divorced and he has no interest in his little daughter, or perhaps he is frail or weak psychologically and is thus a disappointment in some way to the girl, or he might even be sick and not available due to the state of his health. As the girl grows up she feels an overwhelming need for this parent but has no way of fulfilling it for any of the above-named reasons, so a part of her is always empty and yearning for the father. Sometimes she is rewarded with a glimpse of heaven when he is briefly there for her, or simply acknowledges her in ways he normally does not. This transports her into a place of joy she can barely conceive, but it's always just out of her hands, on the one hand because it lasts for such a short period of time, and on the other, because it is never of her own choosing. She cannot bring it about at will, so she craves it even more.

At this point, of course, she is not avoiding any kind of an encounter with the self, she is much too young to consciously be there, but the tenor of her life is paving the way for a future avoidance simply because of these early experiences of yearning and need. As she grows up, she will feel such a need for partners who somehow evoke some of what she felt with her father, and this need will be overwhelming in its intensity, driving away any conscious thought that might lead to seek connection with the self, simply because the need is so strong. When a partner leaves her, or when she has problems with such a partner, she may have reactions that range from panic attacks to physical nausea. And while it is not within the scope of this book to go into greater detail about such neediness, it nevertheless demonstrates the type of drama that is well and active in the lives of many as they avoid the encounter with the Self.

Here again, what is sought is love via an external source (the partner) instead of having understood that if love for the self is not a first, even primordial priority, then love that we seek to replace it - love from an outside source - will forever doom us to failure, even if it is not because we've been abandoned or betrayed, but because the beloved may change in other ways or perhaps even die. If that outside source is your main mechanism for feeling good, then what will you be able to do when the other disappoints you, leaves, or dies? Needing elements from the external world for your basic *inner* well-being is almost always, as we have seen, a formula that spells disaster.

Frantic Activity

A favorite for many highly intelligent and skilled individuals is indulging in frantic professional activity in order to avoid the Self. The tenure-track professor who churns out paper after paper in order to ensure that he does indeed get tenure, or the businessman who has already amassed a fortune, but needs more - *wants more* - because he never feels that what he has is enough to make him feel secure. He may have just as busy a personal life as he has a professional life, perhaps with several ex-wives and offspring from each marriage, and he may indulge in busy relationships with all of these individuals, not to mention other aspects of his social life, but ask him when he spends time with himself and he will most probably give you a look of incomprehension or perhaps even amusement that you would want to know such a thing.

There are people who are simply unable to be alone, it makes them feel uncomfortable, and to a degree this is related to the fact that they don't much know or like the person they are alone with - themselves, and so they continually seek the company of others, often engaging in frantic activity on a social level. They spend their days working, but may stop in for happy hour on the way home, and once home, if they're single, they will, in all likelihood, simply get changed for the evening ahead and spend it out until it's time to come home and sleep in order to be able to repeat the same scenario the next day. *What's wrong with having a busy social life*, you may ask. Nothing - unless it's out of balance. And, as said, also depending on the reasons for which you have such a busy social life.

But let's go back for a moment: it's a somewhat strange way to think about it, but consider this: *do you like the person you are alone with?* If you are alone, there is no one with you - *other than yourself*. So what about it? Do you like the person you are alone with? Do you like yourself? Enjoy spending time with yourself? Look forward to being alone with yourself? Consider yourself good company? Are you *comfortable* with yourself? Would you choose yourself as a friend, if you were not you?

> Loving yourself does not mean being self-absorbed or narcissistic, or disregarding others. Rather it means welcoming yourself as the most honored guest in your own heart, a guest worthy of respect, a lovable companion.
> Margo Anand

Or do you, as many clients have admitted to me, shy away from spending time with yourself? Do you find yourself looking for any activity at all - as the individuals I described above - *in order to avoid being alone with yourself?* Do you find yourself literally running away from any possibility of being alone with yourself? Some clients find themselves experiencing extreme anxiety, even panic, if they have to be on their own, especially if it means being home alone (as opposed to be alone in a public place). They will go shopping, they will eat, watch television, go to parties they don't particularly enjoy, go out on dates with people they don't find very interesting, drink, smoke, take drugs, engage in indiscriminate sex, in short, do anything they can to *avoid the ultimate confrontation with the self.*

Why does this happen? As already indicated in previous sections, we could blame it in part on a culture that places a much higher value on outer, material, social, academic, and professional accomplishment than on the inner quest, where in reality both should be in balance. We could also blame it on a society – and a process of socialization within our family, religious, and educational structures, that does not generally give us appropriate tools to begin the process of self-love. Not egotistical self-love, but healthy, good self-love. If we do not love the self, we will probably not look forward to spending time with the self. *But if we want to love the self, we must also come to know it.* In order to know it, we have to look at it. And looking at it means that at first we may find much we don't like. That's ok. We can deal with all of it bit by bit. But let's begin by looking inside - looking *inside the self*, and not by continually escaping from having contact with the Self by means of any frantic activity.

Amazingly (and this may boggle your mind, if you aren't already aware of it), even psychiatrists, psychotherapists, psychologists, mental health counselors, marriage therapists, family therapists, etc., are generally not required to undergo analysis, or encouraged to delve deeply within. How is it possible that those of us who deal with the human psyche are not required to deal with our own?

Therefore, because we do not find this encouragement to embark on the inner quest, those of us who nevertheless do go ahead with it, frequently find ourselves at odds with the bulk of society, if we are courageous enough to openly speak about it. We are either not understood, we may be mocked, criticized, shunned, and we may ultimately find ourselves ignored, or our friends may simply shake their heads and say or think: *well, that's just his/her thing.*

Getting to know the self, becoming enamored of the self, *finding the beloved within by spending time with the self*, is one of the most liberating things you can decide to do for yourself. All it takes is some curiosity (*how can you not be curious about yourself?*) and desire, and above all, the first step.

A client recently said - as he was undergoing the first few timid steps of getting to know himself - that he did not much like what he was seeing and finding out about himself. He was disgusted and ashamed in some fashion about what he was discovering about himself (although the aspects that were arising, that he was being forced to recognize, were simply human bits and pieces, as we all have them, that may not necessarily be wonderful, but by no means were they terrible either - you might say that as long as you don't begin the journey within, you maintain the possibility of believing in your magnificence in a blind kind of way, but once you start seeing the reality and accepting your own shadow, as discussed earlier, you then begin the *true* possibility for seeing your own magnificence, and this time, in a real way, as opposed to that blind wishful thinking you engaged in earlier).

Said in other words - the process of beginning to know the self is similar to getting to know a friend. At the beginning you only see some of his characteristics. As time passes, you notice he tends to leave a very miserly tip after dinner at a restaurant, and is a very poor loser at tennis. He furthermore has a miserable command of spelling. But you also see how generous he is with his time at a local Big Brothers Association, and how kind he is with the elderly, and he is patient, compassionate, and never judges you. So you begin to appreciate your friend in a balanced way, you see the good and the bad, and you find it all relatively easy to accept. Going back to the client mentioned above for a moment - recognize how poorly our society, our religions, and our educational system prepare us for this process of getting to know ourselves, if an individual from a good background, with a decent education and excellent personal and professional life, at least at first glance, is not aware enough to be able to realize that part of getting to know that self is also getting to know the bits and pieces that are not above par. Do you understand now why we are so afraid of taking the journey within? On some level we know that it means facing ourselves; it means looking at ourselves with brutal honesty, and it means deciding (or so we fear) whether or not we are worth accepting and liking.

Possessions, Positions & Physical Prowess

Avoiding the self comes in so many guises. And of course that means that we are able to deceive ourselves and believe that what we are doing will help us advance in life, or that it is for our health, or for the benefit of our families, instead of acknowledging that we are, in fact, simply using one more ploy to avoid the self.

> Believing in our hearts that who we are is enough is the key
> to a more satisfying and balanced life.
> Ellen Sue Stern

Our possessions, our social and professional positions, our youth, the beauty and fitness of our bodies, are all things that we use to avoid the Self by seeking more of them, or by improving them. We believe that how we feel when we achieve whatever we set out to do in this process, will once and for all make us feel better about ourselves because we earn more money, or move in higher circles, or have gained greater power, or have become thinner, sleeker, bulkier (as in muscles), younger, and so forth.

One of the messages we continually give ourselves as we continue on in this vein is that we are not good enough as we are. We will be worth more - or perhaps *good enough* - if we are recognized and esteemed in sectors of the business world that apply to what we do, or if we win the neighbourhood paddle tournament, or if we are able to acquire a vacation home in the Caribbean and another in a popular ski resort, or if we no longer fly commercial, or if we have the brightest children in the best schools, or if we are the thinnest of our friends, or the most vegan, or the one who runs in all the marathons. In and of themselves, there is nothing wrong with any of these things, but as I've described them, when they are used to make the self feel better without realizing that they keep you from the Self, then they have become substitutes for connecting with the self and beginning to love the Self. Realize that while these privileges, honors, rewards, or toys may be lovely, and may certainly make life more comfortable or prestigious, when they are what essentially give a person a sense of self-esteem, then they are being used for all the wrong reasons - and to a large degree it is our culture that lies at the bottom of much of this.

It's clear that achievement is a positive thing and healthy achievement does indeed work in your favor. It's one of the ingredients that can give you a strong sense of value and esteem. Without a doubt I most certainly encourage people with low self esteem to consider reaching for goals that mean something to them. However, don't forget that just as with the examples I gave earlier of using external success or material wealth to increase low self-esteem, if nothing is changed on the *inner* level, those external achievements tend not to *improve* true self-esteem, as much as *mask* low self-esteem. Further, they may result in enslaving the person who pursues them to achieve ever more power, wealth or recognition.

A super achiever with low self esteem? It sounds more like an oxymoron than anything else. And yet if we take a closer look at what drives the super achiever, we may find precisely a lack of appreciation and recognition of value of the self underlying all that zealous and disciplined effort. What does a person who is driven to achieve success after success actually get in return? A sense of accomplishment, you might say, the satisfaction of having arrived at a sought-after goal, the pleasure of success, and the pleasure of the journey undertaken to get there. All of these possibilities are indeed, correct. And many achievers *achieve* for those reasons. But many others *do not.*

Those others are driven instead by a need for recognition, a need for appreciation, a need for approval, a need for applause, a need for respect from others, a need for - in other words - *an outer admiration, regard, perhaps even deference, and positive reception of the self.* They are driven by this acknowledgment of the self from others, from an *external* source, rather than by the *intrinsic, internal, self-propelled* feeling of achievement we acquire when we are the ones who give approval, love, and admiration to the self.

When the feeling comes from the inside, it is an affirmation of what you *already know and believe* about yourself (or are in the process of beginning to know and believe). When, however, the need for the feeling can only be fulfilled by an outer, external source, then it is because *you do not yet believe in your own value, merit, and worth.* This can be a critical situation for the self, because under these circumstances you are forever doomed to seek what you need by achieving more and more, greater and higher success, in order to assure you will receive the admiration and esteem you require in order to simply feel good about yourself. Said in other words, under such circumstances, you become a slave to external approval and will do whatever it takes to receive it as often as you require in order to feel good about yourself.

The solution to this rather untenable predicament is not as difficult as it may appear at first glance. Often the "comfort zone" is an important factor, understanding by comfort zone that arena of your life where you feel comfortable, and realizing that you may need to step out of it (step beyond your current status quo) in order to acquire self esteem that is self-propelled as opposed to being dependent on receiving it from external sources (that's the part that will make you feel like you are out of your comfort zone, because at the beginning you are unfamiliar with how to be the motor behind your own self-esteem). Another is the realization that you seek *external* approval or recognition by achieving *in order to feel good.* The next step is to realize that *without the external approval* you never feel as good about yourself as *with it.* Next comes the question *why* this might be so and the rather evident answer that it involves your sense of self esteem. If this sense of self esteem were on a healthy level, *you would not need the external recognition*, because then you would offer this sense of recognition *to yourself, by yourself.* And therein lies the final step to the solution: working on your sense of self esteem by *giving to yourself all of the approval and accolades you would give to another* who does or achieves as you yourself do. In other words, *treat, admire, and respect yourself as well* as you would treat your most dearly beloved partner, friend, child, or admired associate. But to be able to do that, as we have seen, you need to begin the process of loving yourself.

Holier Than Thou

Have you ever met someone who does more good for others than you do? Someone who *cares* so much for the poor, hungry, rejected, and downtrodden of this world that his entire being is dedicated in some fashion to helping others? Worthy causes are the prime purpose of his existence. And while he never goes out there to sing his own praises, in other, more subtle ways, he is always at pains to let you know how much he *cares* for those others, how much he *thinks* of their burdens, how much time he dedicates to *easing* their existence, and how much he *tries* to encourage others (such as you, perhaps?) to emulate his ways, even if only a few hours on the weekend. Don't misunderstand - there are people who are genuinely generous with their time, skills, and money and who help others in many and marvelous ways - but some do all this not just to help, but in part as simply one more ruse to avoid the self.

> Where one feels infantile and powerless, impotent and worthless, that is where the damaged child creeps away rejected and forlorn and comes back again with a very dangerous friend.
> Liz Greene

Think of it: the more I see myself as unselfish, the more I can think of myself as a good person, perhaps even superior to or somehow better than many out there who aren't doing a fraction of what I do, and so as a final result this allows me to think well of myself, and to have a measure of self-esteem that hinges on continuing in this vein of goodness and selflessness and superiority. But somehow, you see, it doesn't always work out well that way. Such thinking implies that much is repressed - perhaps such a person is psychologically abusive to his/her family in the privacy of the home, or such a person has a gambling or drug problem, or is a sex addict, or has anger management issues - and as most things that are repressed, these hidden parts of life tend to surface unexpectedly, and when they do, much of the theoretically good work that this person has accomplished, is lost in the damning face of what has now been made public about this other part of the personality.

None of this would happen if there had been an encounter with the self and if in that encounter this individual had begun to supply him or herself with self esteem that arises from within, as opposed to achieving it from how others view him due to - in this case - good deeds, and forcing himself to stay within the confines of the strait jacket of the do-gooder in order to continue receiving praise and admiration from others.

> There is nothing noble about being superior to some other man.
> The true nobility is in being superior to your previous self.
> Hindu Proverb

So the lesson here - in this particular dynamic that serves to avoid the encounter with the self - is not only to realize that by living a life that is - at least in part - a lie, the suppressed or repressed bits will eventually come up and cause a bit of a nuisance, but also that if the distance or the dichotomy between the self that is shown to the outer world (the *persona*) and the self that is suppressed is very large, then what will emerge will often serve to cause embarrassment, or indeed a downfall of sorts for the individual. One is reminded of certain tele-evangelists who fell from grace in the eyes of their audience when sexual dalliances were made public, or embezzlement of funds that should have been destined for the poor and hungry recipients of a charity in an African country for which a high-standing representative of a community had been fundraising. Similarly, one is reminded of renowned political figures on the global scale that have had equally difficult downfalls due, again, to sexual dalliances or even harassment.

We go to these extremes to avoid the encounter
Self - as indicated frequently throughout this chapter - bec
fear discovering what we don't know about ourselves. Have
another look at the section titled 'Frantic Activity' above to refresh
your memory about how people feel initially when they begin to
see the truth about themselves. No one would deny another the
right to have good and bad aspects to the personality, shades of
darker and lighter characteristics, but when it comes to ourselves,
we somehow wish and hope we are all good, all light. Deep down,
however, we know this is not the case, and so we fear the
discovery, and go to the lengths described here in order to avoid
finding out. Unfortunately, this also precludes being able to set off
on the wonderful road that leads us to loving the self, as well as
preventing us the pleasure of our own acquaintance. This is an
excruciating loss that can be avoided by taking some of the steps
offered in this (and many other) books.

Churches, Temples, Mosques, Synagogues & Ashrams

I was raised in a family that was fairly fundamentalist in
outlook. While most members of my family were of an evangelical
bent, some were Catholic, but basically non-practicing. So on one
side I was surrounded by well-meaning and loving people who
nevertheless believed that unless you lived according to the
precepts of their particular set of beliefs, you were wrong, exposing
yourself to damnation and ultimately condemned to be a sinner.
You may understand that I had many people praying for the
salvation of my soul. Despite that, however, books continually 'fell'
into my hands, or people walked into my life that spoke to me of
many other things that were so unrelated to all that surrounded
me, that I often wonder how I did not become hopelessly confused.
But I felt such a resonance with this other way of thinking (that I

espouse in all my books), and it gave me such a sense of vitality and being alive, that I knew that while what I was rejecting on my family's side might be valid and true for them, I *had* to walk in a different direction.

Once I removed myself from all the family pressure, which created not infrequently at best a sense of great discomfort and at worst a terrible sense of guilt or even that I was a bad person, I felt that I was finally able to breathe a sigh of relief. Then I fell in love with a staunch Catholic, who came from a highly practicing family, so once again, while no one tried to oblige me to do anything I did not want to do, I was considered to be someone who walked the wrong road, essentially a sinner, and so I was continually outside my own comfort zone in trying to appease both my inner yearning and all those who surrounded me hoping that I would finally see the light and leave all those other interests and beliefs of mine that were considered wrong, false, or even deluded.

> We will discover the nature of our particular genius when we stop trying to conform to our own or to other people's models, learn to be ourselves, and allow our natural channel to open.
> Shakti Gawain

What soon became clear to me, however, both with my own nuclear family and then the one I married into, was that much of what was going on was simply a case of quite a few people who had bought into a set of beliefs (and I am not judging whether those beliefs are right or wrong) that they had never *questioned.* This made me feel as though they were standing on sinking sand, as I saw, for example, how they quivered in fear of death, in the cases of those who had aged and were ill and dying. If their faith was so pure and strong, and if they believed all that they said, then why did this not give them solace in the hour of their need? I also felt the sinking sand in a very different way, when I saw that some of them and members of the congregations they belonged to, simply did not walk their talk. They were often not compassionate, not kind, but rather, some of them were hypocritical, even downright mean, spiteful, cruel, gossiping, lying, stealing, cheating, and judging. How, I asked myself, could one attend a church service on a Sunday and be pious, so to speak, and then be the way some of them appeared to be, the rest of the week? Because of this I felt even more justified in my desire to leave all of organized religion behind. Of course I realize that all those negative characteristics I've just thrown out there at some of these people, are negative characteristics that many of us share, and certainly, in that *many*, I include myself. But, or so I felt, the difference was, that on my side there was a conscious attempt to avoid posturing, holier than thou attitudes, and hence hypocrisy.

More than that, however, I asked myself what had gone wrong with the system. Organized religion appears to have let so many people down. It seems to have made unthinking parrots of the masses, which, rightly or wrongly, choose not to think about what their religion actually stands for and signifies. If this is really what the churches, synagogues, temples, mosques, and cathedrals are doing to us, then isn't this just another dynamic, dressed in the symbols of the gods these religions represent, to avoid the Self? If everything has been thought out for you, then why think yourself? *Love your brother as yourself, but don't love yourself because that is selfish. Turn the other cheek, but for the sake of peace, let's wage a crusade on the heathens, or a war on those who live behind this border or stand for that belief. If you don't abide by 'my' rules you are a sinner.*

I began to realize that well-meaning and kind people nevertheless were turning into drones of a sort by rote memorization of whatever their particular church had taught them. And furthermore, they turned against each other, because what went on in their heads said: *your* religion is wrong and *mine* is right, and it's also the only one that will take you to heaven, so you had better convert. Instead of learning to think for themselves, instead of learning to love themselves and all others, they were learning to believe that there is only one true church and one true God, and adhering to the narrow vision such beliefs carry with them. In turn, they then seemed to care more about proving to others the rightness of their beliefs, than of understanding about love, living love, sharing love, being love, and ultimately, living the god-like existence that is possible for all of us, if only we begin to venture on the journey within and connect with and love the Self.

I had no answers to my questions, nor did I know how to resolve this dilemma, but I did know that love was a large part of the solution, as was the concept that we are all one. But our churches were not teaching that. Instead, they were telling us that we were only worthy if we upheld the beliefs that someone (generally a decidedly human being, who was also almost always male) had decided were the interpretation of the deity which that particular religion was founded upon. Clearly, I felt, something was terribly wrong. Our faith and our beliefs, even our churches, often gave us comfort and succor in times of need, but mainly they seemed to keep us from connecting to the divine source (Self) within. We were presented with numerous intermediaries who dictated to us what to think and how to live our lives, not only in medieval times, but in many ways even today. Can you think of any religion at all, other than perhaps Buddhism and all its corollaries, that does not set down rules by which the faithful are to abide? What was - in its true origins - something that I believe was truly holy and numinous in nature - nevertheless became degraded to what we see now in the 21st century. Coming closer to the Self is holy, I believe, and furthermore leads people to then be capable of coming closer to and loving others - even the beggar on the street in Mother Teresa style, but being kept from the self, by telling the faithful that loving the self is selfish, or even a sin, is a process that works very much against our best interests. How is it possible that our churches are not aware of this?

Our Beleaguered Partners

This section is an easy one to understand because we all have either been clung to by a partner, or have done the clinging ourselves. Our neediness - or that of our partner - and not recognizing it for what it is, bring us to the final dynamic I'll be discussing in this chapter, that keeps us from the encounter with the self. Neediness and the projections we cast out there in order to find fulfillment with our partners for many of the things we should learn to first give ourselves, as opposed to looking for them in the partner, are topics discussed at length in *The Tao of Spiritual Partnership*, but I will reiterate some of the salient points.

We are socialized into believing that love and love relationships will not only bring us, but that they *owe* us happiness. We are not taught that we are responsible for our own happiness - indeed, when I bring this up with clients, I find they are often, at least at first, not receptive to this idea at all. It means you can't blame others for how you feel, you know. We also believe that if we need someone, it means that we are in love. Nothing could be further from the truth. *Needing* something out there, something that someone else fulfills for me, simply means that I have not figured out how to give it to myself. You could say I've not bothered *learning* how to give it to myself because it is so much easier to make someone else responsible for it. And let me add that those people who *do* work on fulfilling things for themselves, so that they need not go and look for someone to give it to them, are the people you would want as partners. When they love, they do so, not because they need, but because they truly love. Period.

But before we get to that place - where we are able to accept the idea of being responsible for our own happiness, and for figuring out how to fill our own needs - we believe in some fashion that it is our partners who are meant to bring us this elusive happiness. And when that does not happen, it means the relationship is wrong for us, or that the partner has changed, or the partner no longer loves us, or we don't love the partner anymore, and so on. We then - in time - move on to a new partner, but if we didn't learn anything from that first situation, the same kind of thing will happen again, and much to our surprise, we will be with yet another partner who no longer makes us happy. We may think we have such *bad* luck.

This process, of seeking happiness and fulfillment in the partner, is yet another dynamic that keeps us from the Self because *precisely* due to the fact that we believe that that which we seek is out there; *should* be out there, in the guise of our partner, we once again do not begin to apply ourselves to any kind of encounter with the Self. On the contrary, whatever goes wrong or turns out badly, in our minds we believe we have the partner to consider responsible for that. Please don't think I am making snide comments about silly people. *This is how so many of us live our lives* and it applies across all socio-demographic sectors, simply because it has been so reinforced by our culture, and our very parents, teachers and educators, as well as ministers and other religious figures who tell us the same story because they themselves were socialized in similar a manner.

Why are our partners so beleaguered? For the same reason we are *also* beleaguered: we want of them, and they want of *us* what most of us are unwilling to do for ourselves. Taking on responsibility for your own happiness is hard to do for yourself, but nearly impossible to do for another. But why should we? Does it make sense that any one human being should take on the responsibility for the happiness of another?

> Plant your own garden and decorate your own soul, instead
> of waiting for someone to bring you flowers.
> Veronica A. Shoffstall

Chapter 6

Consequences of Not Loving the Self

Your sacred space is where you can find yourself again and again.
Joseph Campbell

It goes without saying that no one becomes aware of the consequences of not loving the self until he is well down the road of not doing so. When realization dawns, or when he is sitting with a therapist, it becomes obvious that poor self-image, lack of good care for the self, spending most of one's waking moments in a fog of blindness, or lack of awareness, having unhealthy needs that substitute so much that the psychologically, emotionally, and spiritually fit individual would have long ago begun fulfilling for him or herself, and serving a master called *you should* are merely indications of the heavy price that is paid for not loving the self. It can always be undone, but as with most habits and ways of living one's life, the more deeply engrained these habits and beliefs are, the more diligently and assiduously one has to work in order to eliminate them.

Allow me to interject some brief comments regarding the subject of neuroplasticity, neurogenesis, and forming new (and better) neural pathways in your pre-frontal cortex. The brain is flexible (that's what we mean by neuroplasticity), and it remains flexible throughout your entire life. It is capable of growing new branches (dendrites) on its neurons that *did not exist before*. Synapses connect neurons among themselves, and as entirely new ways of doing things may arise due to choices you make or interests you develop, new dendrites are created, no matter what your level of education or age may be. By means of those new dendrites (brought into being by new activities you undertake), the creation of new habits becomes possible. This discovery alone set neuroscience into an exhilarated tailspin, as it signified that the aging brain need not be an insipid brain. The brain is also capable of creating new brain cells (which is what we mean by neurogenesis), even though this was rejected until not too long ago, and therefore when you age and lose brain cells, you need not lose brain capacity, always assuming that you are using your brain in an agile manner, always offering it new data, new information, new ways of doing things, or looking at things in a different, out-of-the-box way, and solving problems creatively, because by so doing, you are maintaining the brain in an optimal state for said neurogenesis.

The consequences of not loving the self are, as indicated, due in part to the fact that habits - bad habits, such as expecting to feel good because your partner makes you feel so because you love that person and he/she loves you back - have become firmly engrained. Many readers may notice a sinking sensation in the pit of their stomach upon reading the dreaded words of 'firmly engrained bad habits', because they are so accustomed to also having heard that deeply entrenched habits are very hard to break, and furthermore, that they may require costly techniques (or therapy) to change. Not so! You must first remember the fact that a portion of your brain - the pre-frontal cortex - is a mass of neural pathways - that exist in a given way right now, at this moment in time in your particular brain, but that can be changed depending on numerous factors, such as (but not limited to):

- Where you choose to place your focus and attention at all times.
- How aware you choose to become and be.
- How much responsibility you take for all you feel, think, say, do and how you react.
- How well you have learned to love yourself.

Remaining conscious and aware ultimately signifies that you spend almost all your time in the present, in the now, and that alone will offer you the opportunity of changing many of those deep habits with relative ease.

By taking a closer look at the consequences of not loving the self, or we might say by more closely examining the causes that also create the effects of not loving the self, we can begin to decipher which part of our behavior needs to be modified in order to create conditions that are more conducive to moving ourselves towards loving the self.

Poor Self-Image

We don't love the self because we have a poor self-image, but conversely, we have a poor self-image because we don't love the self. Where does such a self-image come from, occasionally even a maligned and despised self-image, bearing in mind that most of those who suffer from it, acquired this self-image that left so very much to be desired, long before they may have ever heard of the concept of loving the self?

One obvious place to start is by recognizing that we compare ourselves to others. When we're in the sandbox we notice that Johnny has a bigger bulldozer or that Suzy's doll is like the one they show on TV and not like the one my grandma outfitted with knitted booties. Later, we notice that Mike learned how to spell very quickly and that Jennifer always seems to know the answers to the questions the teacher asks. The fact that I can draw animals to perfection seems to pale in the light of all these other amazing, coveted, and admired intellectual achievements of my fellow first and second-graders.

As we fast forward to another point in the development of our growing poor self-image, we find that Rachel's parents have a maid and spend their winter vacation in the Bahamas, while in our family we take a sled out to the hills surrounding the town where we live, and consider ourselves fortunate to be able to slide down in that brilliant and packed snow. We notice that Richard's father owns the local accounting firm housed in that multi-storey building on the corner of Main and Washington, where dozens of accountants are employed, one of them being my father, and we also take note of the fact that Margaret's mother is a painter who exhibits in several major cities, whereas ours is a housewife. We don't pay so much attention to the fact (or perhaps we're less aware of it) that Rachel's mother drinks too much, and that Richard's father's car is often seen parked late at night outside the home of the beautiful young vet that recently opened her practice on the far side of town, and that Margaret's mother seldom seems to have time for Margaret.

So now our poor self-image extends outwards to our parents, who in some fashion don't seem to measure up, and lest you accuse me of making everyone a snob or an aspiring snob, let me remind you that these are the continual messages we receive via mass media, social media, billboards, television shows and just about everywhere you turn. We receive such insidious messages when we're toddlers and we start watching cartoons on TV, and we continue to receive them as we sit in an old people's home in a wheelchair.

Our society has made the message ubiquitous and until someone (we) sits up and takes notice and does something to change it (global, monumental and all-encompassing, or small and grass-roots: any kind of change will do, as long as it grows), nothing will change: *nothing at all*. So the insidiousness of this message of comparison - where I generally come out losing, because I'll always be comparing what I am or what I have, to what I don't yet have or have not yet achieved, or perhaps will never have and will never achieve, because now it is too late - the insidiousness of this message leads to many negative outcomes, only one of which is poor self-image.

> It ain't what they call you, it's what you answer to.
> W.C. Fields

And just to reiterate once more because this point needs to be fully comprehended if you are going to undertake the kind of change that will offer you freedom from this: a poor self-image has such fertile soil upon which it is able to flourish because as long as we are led to believe - and continue to believe - (and literally don't know that we could believe in a different way) that what gives us high self esteem must come from the outside, from external sources, we will never understand the colossal rift between such a belief and the fact that true self esteem must be born, in fact, from the inside, from the individual who gestates it within, and cannot be gained - can never be gained in any real and lasting way - from any outside sources, because self-esteem gained in that fashion will never be true and will never have the ability to reliably endure because it has never become an intrinsic part of the self.

Poor Care

Think about how you treat some of your prize possessions. How about that Jaguar in your garage? How are you treating it? Oh, you don't have one? Well then, how about your Rolex? I'd be willing to bet you take excellent care of it. Don't have that either? The Armani suit? The Gucci bag? The Ferragamo gown? The Vuitton briefcase?

Whether you own any of these items or not, I imagine that if you did, you would take very good care of them - treat them well, in other words. I don't see you throwing a hammer down on the immaculate paintwork of the Jaguar, nor do I see you carelessly leaving the Rolex in the sand as you go for a swim. The suit and the gown would definitely get hung up properly after wearing them, and you wouldn't leave the Gucci bag out in your garden for the humid night air to do its work on it.

So if you take such excellent (and loving) care of all those *special* possessions of yours (even if yours are not the ones I've described with tongue-in-cheek irony), *why don't you take the same kind of good care of yourself?* Particularly, *why do you treat yourself* in ways you would in all likelihood *never* treat a special possession?

We place great value on some of the objects that populate our lives, even if they are not as costly as the ones indicated. Perhaps you are a book lover, and cherish each of those volumes in your library. Perhaps you play the piano and the one standing in your living room is lovingly tuned on a regular basis. Perhaps you play golf and you clean and polish those irons each time you play 18 holes. You get my point. *What is it about us that we do not tend to cherish ourselves?*

One thing is how we do or do not love ourselves, but quite another thing *is how we treat* ourselves. This involves not only the care we give our bodies (quality of food, air, exercise, relaxation, and rest), but also the care we give our mind and spirit (quality of the company we keep, and what we *feed* ourselves with our eyes, our brain; i.e., what do we watch, what do we read, what sort of conversations do we have), as well as the care we take *in speaking to ourselves.* Call this how we 'nurture' ourselves.

Love brings you face to face with yourself.
It's impossible to love others if you don't love yourself.
John Pierrakos

Imagine you are out on the golf course and came in way over par. What words do you sling into yourself, as you berate yourself for the idiot you were for not being able to play better? *Would you speak like that to your young son or daughter whom you are teaching how to play*? Would you not - instead - encourage him to *try again,* saying that next time he has a good chance of doing it a whole lot better? Would you not speak words of positive and proactive support, in order to ensure that he would indeed try those shots again on the most constructive and helpful note possible?

Imagine you have just tried a new recipe and somehow it did not result in quite the mouth-watering gourmet dish you expected. Are you angry at your lack of culinary expertise? Do you insult yourself for being less than perfect? Or do you have an internal conversation that encourages you to try it in another way, or to consult with someone who has greater knowledge than you about the subject, recognizing that *this is the way one learns, by trial and error and by asking questions of the experts.*

What are your mistakes and failures, but attempts at doing something that has not yet quite become a successful part of your repertoire? How did you learn how to drive? Were you perfect from the start? How, for that matter, did you learn how to walk?

I love using this example with my clients. We've all learned how to walk, even though we may not remember it, and many of us either have children that we have observed learning how to walk, or we know children of other people that we have observed in that same process. What happens? Doesn't the burgeoning walker get up from a crawling position by holding on to furniture or the legs, skirt, or trousers of a conveniently placed adult and take a few steps?

Doesn't that child then totter forwards, with a gigantic grin on its face in view of this new world he is discovering? And doesn't he then almost always fall? What happens then? Does he make faces at himself, and shake his fist, and shout (assuming he was not hurt in the fall)? No. I would love to hear from any readers who have ever observed a child reacting like that. On the contrary, the child simply lifts himself up again, and *tries again, supremely convinced that this time it will work.* And if it still does not, the scene is repeated. And repeated and repeated again. Not once does the child think *I'm so bad at this, I guess I had just better leave it, because I will never succeed. I am such a failure.*

And what does the adult that is observing the child do? The moment the child falls, he shouts at him, telling him how stupid he is for not knowing how to walk yet. How on earth could he not have done it perfectly the first time? Don't you see what an idiot you are, he continues to berate the child? *Of course not.* The loving or caring adult opens his arms to the child, encouraging him to get back up on his feet, claps, even if he fell, simply for having tried, and encourages him to try it again, showing him how much he, the adult, believes in the capacity of the child to master this process, and how much he loves the child.

This is love. This is constructive encouragement. This is bringing out the best in another. And this is how we must treat and care for our most valuable asset - ourselves. Caring for the self in loving ways is simply a corollary of loving the Self. Encouraging the self, believing in the self, approving of the self - even in cases of numerous bungled attempts - and also admiring the self for all of these attempts, all forms part and parcel of loving the Self.

Being Lost in the Fog of Blindness

Being blind has much to do with not living on a conscious and aware level. Achieving a state of such awareness has very little to do with intelligence and demographics, and much more to do with having had the good fortune to either hear someone speak about the importance of self-reflection and awareness, or to read about it. Then the concepts can be internalized, and then practiced over and over again, until awareness becomes automatic and second nature, so that *not* being aware is noticed immediately simply because it tends to rob you of much of your inner well-being. In many instances individuals come to such a state of awareness after much pain and distress in their lives, after having hit, so to speak, rock bottom in some way, whether through abuse, loss, illness, abandonment, grief, depression, and a myriad number of other ills to which we - the human race - are susceptible. In those instances, such people pull themselves out of the quagmire, and one of the results is often a high degree of awareness about themselves and the human condition.

What are some of the things that happen as long as we are not aware? One of the major components of blindness is reactivity, and it surely is one of the principal issues that presents itself in most therapists' offices. A person whose buttons are pushed in some fashion by an event or another person, and who then reacts blindly - i.e., without awareness of his inner self - is being reactive. This happens in basically all our relationships - even those with the teller at the bank, or checkout clerk in the supermarket, or the customer service agent at the other end of the phone, not to mention our nearest and dearest. Something is done or said, and we react. Boom! We may regroup later, privately lamenting that we did or said such-and-such, but the next time our buttons are pushed, or we lose patience, or believe we are not being treated properly, we do it again. And that tends to recur over and over simply because we have not yet become aware and conscious enough of ourselves in order to begin making changes. It also happens to a large degree because the ego is in charge, as opposed to the aware self. The ego takes umbrage, the ego needs to be right, and it is the ego that wants to be more, or better, stronger, younger, richer, more powerful, more knowledgeable, and so on

Much has been said in my other books about the question of self-responsibility, and I refer to it once again in this one: if you truly wish to be responsible for yourself, you must consider being responsible for all you feel, think, say, and do, and for how you react under any and all circumstances. Unquestionably, this is very hard for most, especially if they have never heard of it. It's much easier to blame the other, life, or circumstances for your thoughts, feelings, actions, and reactions, as opposed to taking on responsibility for them. Nevertheless, not only is this possible (all it takes is a bit of practice, as well as some intention and attention), but it is also at the core of finding inner peace and freedom, as well as forming a crucial part of the package that involves loving and caring for the self.

Living in a blind fog expresses itself in myriad other ways that create or lead to a lack of inner well-being, and here is just one example: how often have you driven the route you take to work? And then back home again? In all likelihood you do not notice all the buildings you pass, the specific streets, parks, perhaps other scenery (here where I live on the Mediterranean, we see the sparkling, ever-changing sea, the mountains in their green and violet hues, lush, tropical vegetation and flowers, palms that sway in the breeze, and flowering trees that move the senses), and you would tell me something like: "but I have no need to see it all, or pay attention to any of it, because I am familiar with it".

Admittedly, that is partially true, but at the same time it means that during that entire drive you are not conscious of your present moment and of yourself, but are potentially lost deep in thought about something which, if you were to tell me about it, might be an unimportant argument you had with a colleague at work that rankles but you're ruminating about it, or perhaps you're worrying about how to pay the increased mortgage payment this month, or whether your son has finally finished his science project that is due tomorrow. Please don't think I'm implying these topics are not worthy of thought - they are, and perhaps need very careful thought, but what you are doing is probably not a *proactive* kind of thinking about them, but a *worried* mode of thinking (and the difference between the two can not only affect your mood, but also the very matter of the cells in your body and your aging process). And because you are not conscious and aware while you do this, you simply:

- Don't realize that your thoughts have once again run away with you.

- Don't take notice of the scenery you are passing.
- Don't take note of the fact that those very thoughts, because they are paired with worry, or annoyance, or fear, or some other negative emotion, in fact, fuel and create more of that negative emotion in you.

> To be beautiful means to be yourself. You don't need to be accepted by others. You need to accept yourself.
> Thich Nhat Hanh

All of this happens because you are not conscious and aware of yourself and your present moment. Imagine for a second that instead of the above scenario, you focus on the beauty of the old oak tree you pass as you leave the parking lot at work. You breathe in a sigh of contentment because of its magnificence and feel a sensation of well-being course through your solar plexus *despite the tense conversation you just had with a colleague in the elevator* (and the more aware you become, the more *deliberately* you will do this in your quest for a moment of 'now-ness' and inner well-being and peace). As you carry on driving, you continue to focus on whatever is out there that may be beautiful. Should you be driving through inner city streets, this may be a challenge. Perhaps a ray of sunshine illuminates the corner of the street in a particularly spectacular way, or perhaps the warmth of the sun, or the freshness of the falling rain, or the pristine beauty of a snowflake before it melts on your windscreen, are things you could look for.

But in order to remain conscious and aware (in part in order to not allow your thoughts to run away with you; those *worried* thoughts I referred to above; the unhealthy *ruminating*), you can use other methods, as you begin to understand how this process works, and what you can do in order to leave that blind fog in which you have lived thus far. One particularly valuable method is to carry a collection of stimulating, motivational, or inspirational talks (see Appendix D for suggestions) with you in your car in the form of an iPod, MP3 player, CD's, or any other method you can devise that allows you to have a *choice* about what you will fill your mind with as you drive - even if it is only a short five minute drive (as I often do on my way to the supermarket).

> The most terrifying thing is to accept oneself completely.
> Carl Gustav Jung

Think of it like this: do you not choose the food that goes into your mouth? And are you not more and more aware of the importance of avoiding this food or that, and of increasing your intake of fruits and vegetables? You not only know how bad junk food and processed food is for you, you also - hopefully - don't cram your face with it. So you make good food choices based on thoughtful consideration as well as information that is freely available.

Perhaps it's also based on health issues that you are attempting to avoid or improve. *This - having such inspirational or motivational material in your car - is exactly the same thing.* Making choices about what goes into your head as you drive your car - choosing not to listen to a potentially inane radio show filled with mind-numbing commercials, and choosing not to listen to music, because while music can be soothing, it *does* allow the brain to continue churning out those thoughts, or it may provoke *other* thoughts that drain you due to emotions that the lyrics of the songs may evoke as they cause nostalgic, perhaps painful memories to arise. You are aiming to create *healthy* thoughts; you are aiming to create a mindset that allows inner well-being, and you are aiming at creating a habit that will become natural to you, in order that you begin to consider such a state of being *normal*, as opposed to one that you have become so very accustomed to thus far in your life, that keeps you in a state of blind fog, inner distress, and lack of awareness about your choices in life.

And please be aware of this: while these methods are necessary to use as you begin to grow in awareness of the self, once you have achieved in making this part and parcel of your life, you will no longer need 'methods' to keep yourself there because it will have become an ingrained component of your life and behavior. Furthermore, love for your self will have grown to such an extent, that being aware and living an aware life will simply be one of those things that you do as you *care* for yourself. You love yourself far too much to allow yourself to fall into that fog of blindness and reactivity again.

Unhealthy Needs

Allow me to make use of the example about healthy eating from the last section again. We have no trouble understanding that an individual who takes care of him or herself, also makes healthy food choices. He'll exercise. He'll get enough sleep, and in general, will do all those things on a physical level, that show that he takes good care of himself. Another individual who does not take good care of himself simply won't do that, and one of the reasons he doesn't, is because he has unhealthy needs. He may be addicted to sugar, carbohydrates, and or alcohol. He may be addicted to processed and junk food and all the unhealthy chemicals that can be found in them.

Similarly, not loving the self or not knowing *how* to love the self, and quite particularly, not recognizing the importance of loving the self, will give rise to numerous unhealthy needs. We might define an unhealthy need as something you need despite the fact that it isn't good for you. You may even crave it. You may have severe withdrawal symptoms if you are deprived of it. And you may never realize that the reason you are so dependent on it is because it supplies with something you desperately need - to feel good about yourself and to approve of yourself - that you are looking for in all the wrong places, and that you believe can only be obtained externally - from outside of yourself. And the fact that you look to fulfill your need in all the wrong places is emblematic of our culture.

So when we speak about not yet having learned to love the self and therefore unhealthy needs expressing themselves in the person's life as we've seen, here are some of the more obvious needs we would look for:

- gambling
- indiscriminate or even risky sex
- alcohol and substance abuse
- frantic socializing
- continual retail therapy
- power seeking
- workaholic behavior
- achievement or even one-upmanship (materially, socially, professionally academically, in sports, in physique, in youth, etc.)
- eating disorders
- obsession with one's body image
- extreme fitness behavior (as in spending too many hours dedicated to fitness in order to force the body in some specific size and shape)
- being judgmental or critical (judging or criticizing another means one can feel better about oneself by comparison)

But there are other characteristics in the person with unhealthy needs that don't necessarily spring to mind so easily, that tend to involve other people. Here are some of the less obvious indications that we would look for:

- such a person would need to spend all his free time with the love partner, in order to feel good, as opposed to being healthily independent, even when he is in a love relationship

- such a person would need to be 'made' happy by others, as opposed to recognizing that his happiness is his own responsibility

- such a person would need to feel 'needed' by the love partner, in order to feel good, as opposed to understanding that being needed takes away - at least a part of - healthy freedom in a relationship

- such a person would need to feel he needs the partner in order to believe he is in love, as opposed to understanding (just as in the statement above) that being needed takes away - at least a very crucial part of - healthy freedom in a relationship

- such a person would need to have his needs fulfilled by the partner (for example, feeling protected, safe and secure, or feeling that he is accompanied and not alone), as opposed to learning how to fulfill his own needs

- such a person would need to blame others for how he feels, for example, when difficult or painful things happen, as opposed to taking responsibility himself

- such a person would need to be right when an argument arises, because by being right, he would be able to feel better about himself (as pointed out earlier, this is the work of the ego)

As you can see, most of these points indicate a relationship between these needs and feeling good. In other words, the person who has unhealthy needs *uses* those needs (in fact, such a person *needs* to use those needs) in order to fulfill a requirement of extraordinarily high significance: feeling good in general, and most particularly about him or herself. He does not know how to make himself feel good *on his own*, without others or without material things or external events or achievements, because he does not yet know how to love himself, and so he has unhealthy needs (as an alcoholic needs alcohol) in order to manage to feel good. And all of this is almost always unconscious, hence creating more of that blind fog I referred to in an earlier section.

> The deepest principle in human nature is the
> craving to be appreciated.
> William James

This need for another or for certain things or events in order to feel good about yourself - just like a substance would - may create dependence, although in this case the dependence is generally more about another person - the one who does whatever it is that you need in order to feel good - than about anything that can be ingested. Evidently such dependence creates a whole other series of issues that arise when the other person leaves you, or is no longer willing to comply with doing whatever it was to ensure that those needs of yours get filled. As we have seen, the individual with unhealthy needs may - at such a point - experience panic and anxiety attacks, hysteria, nausea, and other physical and psycho-somatic reactions due to something that is very similar to acute withdrawal symptoms another person who suffers from substance abuse would experience. And again, all of this can be laid at the door of not knowing - or never having learned - how to love the self.

It is often at this critical point - when the person has been abandoned or otherwise rejected by the other who up to now had been fulfilling crucial needs - that someone in my profession receives a call and an appointment is made. So far so good, because if the crisis acts as a catalyst for growth for the person with the unhealthy needs, then the crisis has served an excellent purpose. Unfortunately, however, due to many different reasons, including the manner in which our culture socializes us - as already referred to in earlier chapters, from the time we are born to the time we die, unless we wake up and begin to think for ourselves - we are prone to believing that when things of this nature happen (someone ditches us, for example), that we chose badly, that we had bad luck, that the other person is somehow to blame, and we *rarely or never look at ourselves* in this process. Therefore we suffer tremendously, and the anxiety or panic attacks, as well as the nausea or hysterics may be treated by a well-meaning doctor or psychiatrist with psychotropic medication for depression, anxiety, panic attacks, or insomnia, and we are well on the road to another kind of dependence or even addiction and have, therefore, never faced the true underlying issue which is that we do not love ourselves.

It's not about blaming the self for the way the relationship that no longer fulfills our needs played itself out, but about *recognizing* that blaming anyone or anything will not bring us closer to closure or a solution, and it certainly won't make us feel better in the long run. Nor is it about choosing 'better' partners, weighing the pros and cons more carefully, and so on, nor about keeping our hearts firmly under lock and key so that we are not abandoned, hurt, or otherwise mistreated again at some future point, but indeed about recognizing that our partners offer us a glimpse into our own selves, even our souls, by what they reflect back at us, and what this reflection of ourselves can teach us, and how we can grow thanks to it (this topic is the main theme of my book *The Tao of Spiritual Partnership*). And so this glimpse that we are offered through the vagaries and roller coasting ups and downs of the relationship can be used as a tool - as an infinitely precious gem - indeed, we can choose to make of it a *tao*, a path that can aid us in growth, progress, and transformation as individuals into becoming more of what we can be.

This is the prize, this is the place at which we can arrive thanks to our unhealthy needs, but this has a stern taskmaster as it requires that we become aware, that we take complete responsibility for the self, and that we begin the process of consciously loving the self.

Serving the Master 'Should' & Living Other People's Lives

Our lives are filled with helpful suggestions couched in the language of 'you should do this or become that'; 'you should study here or go there', and many of these suggestions come from well-meaning people in our lives who may even love us. Whether their suggestions are valid or not, is not as important to the outcome of our lives, as what we do with the advice that I have labeled the "*you should's*" of our lives.

Let's have a look at another typical version of these "*you should's*" that enter our lives in much more insidious ways than the helpful suggestions named above:

- you should be successful
- you should be rich
- you should be famous
- you should be young (or look young)
- you should be thin
- you should wear this

- you should carry a handbag with that label
- your briefcase should be made by that firm
- you should belong to that political party
- you should not marry outside of your religion, ethnicity, etc.
- you should be invited to that dinner
- you should choose your friends from that section of society
- you should read this book, or that newspaper
- you should drink this wine
- you should be familiar with the cuisine of that country
- you should never raise your voice or laugh too loudly

Much of this sounds dreadfully superficial, and yet we all know to what extent we are influenced by thoughts or guidelines of this nature due to the daily barrage of input we receive from not only the media, but also from the people in our lives.

> Too many people overvalue what they are not
> and undervalue what they are.
> Malcolm S. Forbes

So here is the question you need to ask yourself: are you *aware* of how much of your life is decided by these (and other) *you should's*? Do you *know* that you can make other choices that may, in fact, be far superior and certainly more beneficial for you, offering much greater freedom, as long as you are inherently willing to be *different*? Have you carefully *examined* which of all your choices are indeed *yours*, and which are often based on what YOU think you *should do*?

This is all related to how much and how well you love yourself. The *should's* of your life will loom much more largely in direct relation to your lack of love, because they too, are another way of finding love, approval, and acceptance, and of avoiding that dreaded monster that always lurks: disapproval and rejection.

For that matter, how much of your time - your life - is spent living your life for others? What is it you really care about? What gives you a wonderful sense of inner well-being?

- Is it what others think of you?
- Is it about how important they perceive that you are?
- Or how popular you are? Or the people you rub shoulders with, or are on a first-name basis with?
- Is it about being seen at certain places, restaurants, or parties?
- Is it about wearing certain kinds of clothes?
- Or perhaps about how your home is furnished? Or its location? Or what sits in your driveway, or in the berth at the marina?
- Is it about your position at the firm? Your bank account? How well you play golf?
- Is it about how often you attend yoga class, how advanced you are, or whether you visit this ashram or that one in India?

Somehow I don't believe *any* of the above gives you that wonderful sense of inner well-being, and yet, that is what so many of us do - living a life for the sake of others, with respect to how we are perceived by all those others based on any of the above benchmarks.

Why on earth do we do this? How do we allow ourselves to be lulled into this manner of thinking that has nothing whatsoever to do with real inner well-being and is totally disconnected from our birthright to live well, in joy and filled with love and acceptance for ourselves? Is it because of our childhood? The manner in which we are taught to give importance to our appearance and the *toys* we have, or the toys *our parents* have? If that forms a true part of the explanation, please give your parents, assuming they are alive, a copy of this book and ask yourself some very serious questions about how you are handling the raising of your own children. Or is it because of the all-pervasive influence of mass media? We can't discount it, and we often discuss it, so why not give it its proper place in our lives - a place that *we* control, as opposed to the media controlling us by whatever it is they are trying to make us believe, purchase, or bend our figurative knee to.

Don't misunderstand: I'm not stating there is anything wrong with the above: having lovely things, knowing popular, famous or powerful people, or going to beautiful or even exclusive vacation spots. What I'm suggesting is that it makes no sense to live our lives for the sake of others, for how they perceive us *for the sake of the place these things have in our lives*.

Think about it: are *you* the one who makes you happy, or does a *thing* do so? In the case of the former, it is safe to assume that you are free, but in the case of the latter you are dependent on the existence of that *thing* in your life, so you are *not* free. *It is up to you because it is a choice you make every day, all day long* and within its tapestry lies the answer to how much you are going about the process of loving the Self.

Chapter 7

That Seemingly Insurmountable Roadblock: Your Past

By letting it go it all gets done. The world is won by those who let it go. But when you try and try the world is beyond the winning.
Lao Tzu

We all want joy and somewhere inside we all know that without growth we don't advance forward in a good direction. So what we need to understand is short and sweet: if you refuse to give up your past, you prevent a good portion of your life *now* - the life you are living in this present moment - from containing joy and allowing growth to take place.

Here is what happens: when you think of whatever it was in the past that was painful, or hurtful, or created anger or resentment or bitterness, you are thinking about that *now*, right? It's not yesterday, it's not tomorrow - your thought takes place *now*. But this very moment that you are living now: this *now* is a long time (or at least *some* - chronological - time) removed from whenever it was that 'it' (and you probably have many 'its') happened. So that means that you spend a lot of your time in the past - at least in your thoughts and emotions. That means that all the time you spend there - in the past - you aren't here and now because you are not *present*. And how do you expect to be filled with joy and growing forward in a positive direction if you aren't here and now?

You might not even be looking for the past in your thoughts, but it comes to you unbidden. How? Here are some typical and simple examples of stimuli that can easily evoke the past to most of us:

- Music: imagine you are driving in the car, enjoying an exquisite day, and a song starts playing that is full of bitter-sweet nostalgia for you. It transports you into the exquisite glory and wrenching pain of a past relationship. Suddenly you are no longer enjoying the gorgeous day; on the contrary, you are re-living parts of the magnificence of that past relationship, and then you are swept up into the pain of other pieces of it. By the time you reach your destination, you not only no longer feel as wonderful as you did when you began your drive, but you no longer remember the actual drive - all because a song was played on the radio.

- Smells, perfumes, aromas: imagine being introduced to a stranger at a cocktail party. Imagine you are a woman, and the stranger is a man, and as you come in a bit closer to say hello, or as you touch cheeks, as we do in so many countries, you get a whiff of his cologne. It is your father's cologne. Immediately, in some fashion, you either associate the stranger with your father, or you go into a memory of the past, perhaps of you sitting in your parents' bedroom, chatting with your father as he splashed on the cologne, and that memory takes you to another moment with your father when he told you he was leaving your mother and you because he had met another woman. Now the cocktail party is tinged with that memory, the feelings it evoked, and after you get home, you may find you scarcely remember any of the conversations you had while you were there - all because of a cologne.

- Movies with specific scenes: these can have a similar effect on you as the above, and you may find that you frequently are attracted to movies that cause you to relive the emotions of certain parts of your life. Think about it: which kind of movie evokes the strongest emotions from you, and how are they related to portions of your own personal history?

Something happens when you access painful memories - whether you access them for simple, everyday reasons, such as those mentioned above, or whether it's because you *tend* to think about certain events that occurred in your past. There is an energetic connection to the memory as it arises, and there is a familiarity about the pain that the memory evokes. The reason there is familiarity - obviously - is because you have probably thought about this many times and each time you do so, you make the memory of the event more powerful, the neural pathways that connect you to that event are made stronger, and hence it becomes progressively harder for you to stop the floodgates of the memory opening more and more. Yet, that is precisely what you are going to have to do if you want to let go of your past.

That's basically it. You need to get this into your head and heart. You need to practice moving away from the past whenever your thoughts and emotions take you there. It's the only way you will create greater joy and growth in your now. And in order to practice, you need to be conscious and aware. You need to love yourself. You need to want it for yourself. And if you so do, then each time you catch yourself going off into the past (and this will require vigilance, since most of the time you go off into the past blindly), you will consciously *choose* to remain in the present by focusing on something here and now, perhaps something of beauty. And you do this in order to decrease the size and strength of the neural pathway in your brain that habitually pulls you into the past. Do it every day several times and very quickly you'll see results because you'll notice you spend less time in the past and your present time elongates. And your joy increases. (If you haven't already done so, look over the *mindfulness walk* described in Chapter 4 and also referenced in Appendix B, as well as the brief beauty and gratitude exercise in Appendix A).

Cellular Energy Binds Your *Now* to Your *Then* & the Magical Circle

Consider for a moment what happens when you think about a painful event in your past. If it's about a matter that you have not yet laid to rest, and if it concerns someone or something that caused you a great deal of distress or suffering, it makes sense that as you think about the event or the person that created the event, you experience emotions. Those emotions create energy in you on a cellular level. If you doubt that last statement, I invite you to look at some of the work of cellular and molecular biologists such as Bruce Lipton and Candace Pert. In her book *Molecules of*

Emotion, the latter affirms - based on her research - that every thought creates a molecule, so when you experience emotions, those emotions create energy in you on a cellular level and have the power to influence your cells.

On a different level, however, there is another kind of energy that is created causing you to feel bound to that past event that provoked pain. You are bound to it energetically because it still has power over you since you have not yet resolved it and because you have not yet forgiven.

Getting over a painful experience is much like crossing monkey bars. You have to let go at some point in order to move forward.
Unknown

Perhaps you were abused in 1972 by a friend of your parents, so whenever you think about what happened over 40 years ago, you feel rage, shame, and sorrow, and so a part of you *is* and *remains* there in that place and time, due to the emotional energy you expend as you think about it. Perhaps in 1985 you were bullied, so whenever you think about what happened nearly 30 years ago, you feel anger, and so a part of you *is* and *remains* there in that place and time. And perhaps your partner betrayed you by sleeping with your best friend, so whenever you think about what happened to you 20 years ago in 1993, you feel tremendous pain, sadness, and resentment, and so a part of you *is* and *remains* there in that place and time.

By these examples, you can see how many parts of you are not *present*; how many parts of you are literally living in the past, at the time of those events, and depending on *how much* of you is invested in maintaining that pain from the past alive, the part of you that is actually living now in the present, may be quite small, compared to all of the energy you exert in your past. This is crucial to your understanding of self-love because as long as you allow such a state of affairs to continue, you simply are not loving and caring for yourself.

Think of your past pain as a physical wound or compare it to how you behave when you break a bone. Clearly, when you injure yourself in some fashion, you have it seen to, or you take care of it yourself. One way or another, you do your utmost to cure it. Then, once you have passed that stage, you may - occasionally - refer to it, as in: 'oh, yes, 2012 was the year I broke my wrist', or: 'I was cutting onions to make a salad for the dinner to celebrate John's 48th birthday, and the knife slipped and I almost cut off the top joint of my index finger'. But other than it being a story that you relate, you tend neither to dwell on it in the telling of the story, nor in the experiencing of any negative emotion from that past event. It was an injury you suffered, it healed, and now you are well. Period.

Therefore when you consider how much of your energy lives in the past due to emotionally unresolved painful matters that occurred then, you come to realize that unless you liberate and free up that energy, the part of you that lives in the present is a fraction of what you truly are. Just imagine what you might be able to accomplish if *all* of you were living here and now!

The fact that in order to do this you must *want* to love and care for yourself enough so that you are capable of achieving it, must be clear to you by now. If you don't care for yourself, you allow such a state of affairs to continue, but as you begin to understand that loving the self implies taking care of all aspects of your life, you recognize this, realizing how paramount it is to very much include specifically those aspects that *carry on causing pain*. The more you care for yourself in resolving past issues, the more you give yourself an unambiguous message that you are walking down the road towards loving the self. You will no longer use those bits of you that live energetically in the past by holding on to those old wounds, to tell yourself and others that that is how you define yourself. You will no longer want that to be part of your identity. You will no longer use any past issue as an excuse to explain why you are unable to accomplish anything at all in your present life. And *not* doing any of these things will make you feel immeasurably better about yourself, and the more you feel better about yourself, the more you love, respect, and approve of yourself. It's a bit like a vicious circle, except that in this case there is nothing vicious about it - on the contrary, you might say it's a *magical circle* that continues bringing in more and more love for yourself.

By untying your present from your past you begin to unravel so much that stands between you and your capacity to love yourself. I can simply not emphasize this enough. So many clients come to see me and many colleagues all over the globe, insisting that their past *cannot* be thought of differently, because what happened was simply too difficult, too painful, and too traumatic. For all intents and purposes they want to hold it in place. Therefore, as you can imagine, such a client essentially wants to talk about the trauma based on the belief in its importance. Generally, however, this is a grave mistake. Talking about the past is not the mistake, but talking exclusively about the past, regurgitating it, reliving it, revisiting it, over and over again, to see what further kernel can be gleaned by once more going over the pain - *that is the mistake*.

You see, if you are invested in keeping your past alive because that is how you identify yourself, or because that is how you tell yourself you give it (the pain) its due, believing that if you let it go, it would mean it had not been important, in such a case, you will simply not be willing to begin to talk about how you can consciously choose to change your present by beginning to leave your past in the past. That is the crux of the matter. And until you come to the realization that choices can always be made, and that the choices that are made signify whether the past can be laid to rest or not, and hence also signify whether you can *finally* begin to love the self, nothing will change, and you will not find peace, will not find well-being, will not find harmony, and will not find joy, nor love. Do this for yourself, do it because you want freedom.

The Past Won't Ever Change, but You Can Change the Present

You were lied to, you weren't invited, you were ignored, you were betrayed, you were humiliated, you were abandoned, you were laughed at, you weren't accepted, you were considered lacking, you felt left out and defeated.

Some, if not all of these things have happened to most of us. They certainly don't feel good. Thinking about them may feel nearly as bad as it did when they were occurring. And even thinking about them a long time later, especially if you feel that what happened was very important, still feels nearly as bad as when they were occurring. Therefore, thanks to your *thoughts*, you willingly (you *do* choose your own thoughts, don't you?) go through the experience over and over again.

Note: I *know* that most do not, in fact, choose their own thoughts, hence I have written this - and my other - books, in the hope that they serve as maps so you may learn to be the one who is consciously in control of and choosing your thoughts).

But if you decide, as soon as you can after the event that you will no longer give it energy by thinking about it, then you don't have to go through all of the above over and over again. It doesn't mean that what happened is OK, nor does it mean that it was in any way or fashion good, but it *does* mean that you can choose to let it leave your memory in a conscious way by being aware of the fact that loving yourself and being accountable to yourself about your inner well-being implies letting go of that which no longer serves you. Confucius said: *To be wronged is nothing unless you continue to remember it.* I would add that to be wronged is nothing unless you continue to insist on thinking about it, once the memory enters your head.

Clearly, you probably won't forget, nor is it necessary to forget. It's just necessary to be conscious enough to make good choices, and in this instance a good choice is to not belabor the past, to not continue thinking about something negative that happened, because to do so is to fuel the flame. I'd like to use another physiological and biological analogy here: childbirth. Many women have a very difficult time giving birth, and indeed, go through a great deal of pain. Nevertheless, even of those who have full use of their free will, many voluntarily choose to have more than one child, knowing full well that it may create more suffering or pain. Generally speaking, these women do not dwell on the discomfort or pain they went through, if and when they recount the story of giving birth. They don't repeat over and over again (even to themselves, in their private thoughts) how painful and difficult it was. They have simply let it go. We can take a very positive lesson from this.

Another way of thinking about how you can change your past so that your present is different, is by considering why you react the way you do on certain occasions. For example:

- Why do you get upset when a store clerk does not come to help you immediately?
- Why do you react coldly when you are told by your boss that something you have done needs rectification?
- Why do you feel anxious when you are preparing a report despite the fact that you know you'll be able to complete it

well before the deadline, and with ease, because you've done this type of report before?

- Why does your stomach tense when you need to ask your husband for money, or tell your wife that you've just purchased a high-end set of golf clubs?
- Why do you think you feel insulted when the person in the car with you tells you to watch out for oncoming car, even though you've already seen it, and even though you have proven yourself to be an excellent and careful driver over many years?
- Why do you feel intimidated by haughty maitre d's?

These and many other examples I could mention are frequently the red flag of something that has some kind of power over you, *of splintered fragments from your past that have power over you and therefore make you feel a certain way.*

Events and feelings connected to those events from your past may be in charge of parts of your life because you have not yet come to terms with whatever it was that happened. And coming to terms with something often implies *forgiving someone from your past in order to disconnect yourself from the energetic connection you still have with the feelings that such an event evoked in you.* Without the process of forgiving, you not only continue to feel unwanted emotions whenever you remember the past event, but, and this is even more important, *you continue to react in ways that are no longer pertinent to your life, due to your emotional connection to that past event, even when you are not consciously aware of the past event.*

So when you react coldly when your boss has some minor constructive criticism about something you have presented him with, it may be connected to the time your father criticized a beautiful painting you had just drawn for him when you were eight, telling you that lions did not really look like that, and that in Africa, skies could not have that impossible color. When he said those thoughtless words to you, his young child, it hurt you so much, that to protect yourself, subconsciously you covered up the hurt with coldness, to help you not to feel it the same way. This protective mechanism is still in place now, and may work against your best interests by your reaction with your well-meaning boss. Hence, we say, *you are controlled by this fragment*. Being controlled by fragments from your past means several things:

- You are not totally aware of everything that is going on, because these fragments *cause you to react in ways that are not part of free choice, they happen because you are in the dark about them.*

- Hence you are not in control of your reactions (remember you can't control what happens to you, but you can absolutely choose how you react to events, *but only if you are totally aware*).

Frequently you can become aware of *splintered fragments having this power over you* if you begin to pay close attention to exactly how you feel at *all* times, not only emotionally and psycholgocially, but also physically. So if you notice a downward spiral in your feelings when certain things happen, you might be on to a clue about one of your fragments. Also, very particularly, you should notice when your solar plexus (stomach area) begins to clench or feel uncomfortable. That is *always* a clue that something is going on that is not right. It could be that someone is behaving with you in ways that are not acceptable, and that you need to check out your boundaries, or it could be that you are about to have a reaction to something that is the result of one of your fragments from the past, and the reason your stomach is clenching, or your heart is pounding, is because *it is directly connected to something that caused you great pain, or upset of some kind when you were younger.*

Discovering these fragments from your past and their - heretofore unknown - impact on your present life, will take you down the road to inner growth and above all, *inner freedom.* (Note: on occasion these fragments will come to light when carrying out the time-line exercise described in Chapter 4 and further illustrated in Appendix C).

I've often wondered if the people whose lives are filled with bitterness and resentment could just see *for a moment* what their lives would be like *without* that bitterness and resentment (and the ensuing pain), whether they would then take the necessary steps towards *making the freedom-giving choice* of putting the bitterness and resentment behind them. Because that is really what it's all about: making a different choice.

It's not so much about being compassionate towards the person (or institution) that did whatever it was; it's also not so much about letting bygones be bygones.

Much more than that it's about recognizing that you can continue to identify with whatever it was that threw your life out of balance at some point in the past (whether that was yesterday or a quarter of a century ago), and that event caused you much pain then, which is why the subsequent bitterness and resentment arose, *or you can decide now that you simply no longer are - nor want to be - that person. So you decide that you choose to be a person without bitterness and resentment for yourself;* for your own good; for your own inner freedom and growth. And particularly in order to *make space inside of you* in order that you may live your life more fully.

As you choose to turn your back on the bitterness and resentment, you no longer need to use up energy - *psychic energy* - (psychological energy) to maintain those feelings. By removing that *wasteful use of your energy,* you now have more 'space' inside of you, and therefore your energy can be channeled towards totally different, *life-giving* endeavors.

It's about forgiving and it's also about getting your power back, and furthermore, about getting your *whole self* back. It's about life meaning and how much that is a *life-giving* force in your existence. More than anything, it's about you, and your love for yourself.

Important life-changing lessons can also be learned by understanding the concept of the pain body and how things seem to *stick* to you emotionally if you don't make a conscious effort to free yourself of them. You may believe you have this business of forgiving others down pat but when it comes to forgiving *yourself,* things look somewhat different. Perhaps you have been remembering:

- Your mother's request when you were 16 to stay in with her on a certain night because she wasn't feeling very well, but you simply wanted to go out and party (you are now in your mid-40's), and of course you know you were such a *selfish* daughter/son.
- Your eldest child's nightmare when she was seven (she is now 29), that you paid little attention to, and you know you did not make her feel safe that night the way a *good and caring* mother/father would have.
- When you weren't nice to the cat on that day last spring because you were so angry at your partner, that you took it out on the cat and yelled at the poor little thing and scared it, and it ran away and never returned, perhaps never

finding a new home, and so you know you were just so *horrible.*

- The fact that you cheated on that *vital* exam that made all the difference to receiving the offer at that top-tier firm right out of law school, and since then you think of yourself as *the lowest of the low.*
- The look in your partner's eyes when he/she realized you had lied that day that you can never forget, and you know you can never be forgiven - not by others and certainly not by yourself.

So, when these (and other examples) arise in your mind, rather than forgiving yourself, you move into the pain body (a term I often borrow from Eckhart Tolle), and in the pain body you *revel in your loathing of yourself*, in the pain you feel for having let that person (or animal, or school, or firm) down in that way, and you go over and over and over the event, each time sinking into deeper pain and disgust and moving farther and farther away from forgiving yourself.

People have a hard time letting go of their suffering. Out of a fear of the unknown, they prefer suffering that is familiar.
Thich Nhat Hanh

But it's precisely there where you must stop, just before you descend into the pain body, and *regain a conscious focus on what you are doing, becoming first and foremost aware of your thoughts*, and to then make the conscious decision that you will not go down there. You realize that going down there means you are actually allowing yourself to go to a pity party, where you get to pity that horrible thing that you are, *as opposed to taking the very conscious step of not going there, and then, with a great deal of awareness beginning the newly conscious process of forgiving yourself.* You do this by intending it. By telling yourself each time you go to those places that you intend to forgive yourself. And then you move on. Preferably into gratitude (also see Appendix A), because that moves you into the present. It's a process. It has to be done over and over. But it can be done and it works. So start now. Today.

Know That Forgiving is For You ... *Not* for the Other

The concept that forgiving is for you and not for the other is very hard - almost unmanageable - for many, many people. Somehow the thought that if you forgive, you are condoning, or in some way resting importance from the magnitude of whatever it was that happened, lies foremost in most people's mind and heart. And as we have already seen, it furthermore brings up the issue about the fact that if you let it go, where will your identity go? In some fashion your past pain has identified you for many years. It is how you explain yourself to others. You frequently bring up the bad bits quite early on in a relationship with someone new because this is such a big part of who you are. Your wound identifies you. Your wound gives meaning to your life. Your wound helps you explain yourself. But simultaneously, your wound also keeps you from moving forward. Your wound retains you in stagnancy. Your wound retains you in pain. And your wound often is the reason why you think of yourself as a victim.

Therein lie many of the reasons why it's crucial that you begin to recognize that when you forgive someone - no matter what awful thing they may have done to you - that you are doing it for yourself and not for the other. Forgiving is first and foremost about you.

Here's a snapshot of what happens as long as you don't, won't or believe you can't forgive: your mind goes to the event, or to the person who perpetrated the event. That part is the memory of what happened. In and of itself, a memory need not be a bad or painful thing. But if you have not yet forgiven, the memory begins to take on a life of its own. In fact, it has had a life ever since the event occurred, assuming you have been thinking about it since then.

Here is a typical sequence of thought and feeling forms as they happen once you think about it:

- You remember the event.

- Your self-dialogue almost immediately consists of painful thoughts, resentment, anger, sorrow, or grief. It may also include thoughts about the fact that you believe you are a victim.

- You begin to go over the events that occurred or words that were said in minute detail. This is very easy since you have done this dozens, hundreds, perhaps even thousands of times already. The neural pathways in your pre-frontal cortex associated with this process have become strongly formed into masses of connections that are inextricably intertwined and that grow thicker and tougher each time you think of the event and experience a resurging of the same emotions.

- Now your feelings arise according to the self-dialogue and the revisiting of events that just took place in your mind.

- In all likelihood, none of this is under your conscious control, i.e., it begins with the memory and you follow the thread more or less as described, as though you were following the directions of a theatre script. You yourself have 'walked' yourself into this place, into this position, and into this 'learned' behavior due to repeating it more or less as described over and over again over potentially many years of your life.

- The feelings that have arisen are a direct cause not of the event or memory of the event, but of your self-dialogue about it because you have not yet taken the decision to forgive. If you had, your self-dialogue would have changed and hence your memory, as stated above, of the event, would no longer have the power to affect your emotions in this self-damaging way.

At this point it is critical to understand that there is an energetic connection between the memory and your feelings. One (the memory) creates the other (the emotions) as though an electric cable connected the two. This energetic connection will remain in place as long as you do not forgive. Over the years it may continually grow stronger. As it does grow stronger, you will consider yourself more and more justified in feeling the way you do and - more importantly - in identifying yourself with all the painful emotions. *This happened to me*, you say, *and it's impossible to forgive and forget*, may be part of the message that runs through your mind over and over again.

It is just as crucial to understand what you can do about a 'repeating' memory. As pointed out in many different parts of this book (and my other books), being self-responsible implies taking care of your inner state of being. In order to even be able to begin to do that, you must consider how your thoughts pop in and out of your head and you would do well to learn how to be in charge of those thoughts, as opposed to allowing them free rein over your mind. This subject has been dealt with in depth in both my other books and in many freely-available articles on my website and blogs, but suffice it to say here that if you begin by avoiding random music on the radio when you drive your car, that may bring up memories, you are already beginning this process of taking charge of your thoughts. If you furthermore practice the brief gratitude exercise (Appendix A), and the mindfulness walk (Appendix B), and begin listening to inspiring talks (find some samples in Appendix D) in your car and in other occasional moments (even just 10 minutes) every day, you will come a long way towards the goal of being in charge of your thoughts very quickly.

Another relatively simple thing to do about 'those' memories is to decide to keep yourself as conscious and aware as possible and then, when they arise, you will have a brief self-dialogue that goes something like this (note that this is only possible if you have, indeed, remained conscious):

- OK, here I go again with the memory from which I wish to disconnect myself.
- In order to do so, I have to pay more attention to this new self-dialogue I'm now having, rather than the old one that wants to pull me back down the same road I always take when this memory arises.
- The old way of talking to myself about this memory is still very strong. I'll have to watch my thoughts very closely. (See all the Appendices mentioned above).
- I'll have to use all my conscious muscle power to keep myself from going there.
- The most important part of the new self-dialogue is that I intend to forgive. I may not be able to do so fully yet, but I intend to do so and with that thought I consciously choose to focus elsewhere as opposed to continuing down my typical path of painful and victim-type thoughts connected to the past event.

- The reason I want to do this is very important - I want to disconnect from all the negative feelings this memory gives me.

- This isn't something I'm helpless about. I'm not impotent about it either, and I can change it by remaining conscious.

- Another significant reason to stop talking to myself the old way about this memory and starting to talk a new way is because this is how that old process begins to erode, just like old highways that fall into disuse when the super highways started being built. The more my old process connected to the self-talk, the memory and the negative emotions begins to erode, the more quickly I'll be able to disentangle myself from those emotions each time the memory arises.

- When that happens the memory will still be there but I'll be able to briefly think about, the way I might think about what I had for breakfast yesterday and the memory will no longer have power over me and won't be able to fling me into a tailspin of difficult emotions.

- When that happens, I will truly have disconnected energetically from the memory and will be free of the difficult emotions.

You will find yourself dueling with your ingrained habits as you attempt this, and it may become a duel of Titans, because this is such a firmly-trodden path in your heart and psyche, as opposed to the new pathway you are attempting to hack though the jungle of your painful memory. Do remember that the new pathway will gain visibility, strength and shape as you do this over and over, each time the memory erupts into consciousness.

At the risk of repeating myself, the reason this happens, the reason you continue to feel those terrible emotions when you think about the past, is because the energetic connection is alive and well. As long as you do not forgive, that is how it will be. And that is why forgiving is all about you and not about the other person.

> In the process of letting go you will lose many things from the past, but you will find yourself. It will be a permanent Self, rooted in awareness and creativity. Once you have captured this, you have captured the world.
> Deepak Chopra

You see, until you forgive, you will not lessen the energy that swirls around the event. But by forgiving, as you will come to read in the next section, by intending to do so each and every time you think of the person or event, by gradual degrees the energy - and the emotions connected to it - will lessen and ultimately disappear. This is a gift you give yourself and each time you work at it, by consciously intending to forgive, you are showing yourself that you love yourself.

Intending to Forgive

"*Never!*", say some. "*I can't*", say others. "*How can I?*" says another group. "*What was done to me was just too terrible to be forgiven*", say most.

Let's examine that last statement. Without a doubt whatever it was that was done to you was bad. We can't change that. Child abuse, child neglect, abandonment, betrayal, domestic violence, false promises - the list goes on and on, and all of us have a story to tell. But if you agree that what happened in the past cannot be changed, you're on the right track.

But now you say: "*It can't be changed, but it was so terrible, that I will never - in my whole life - be able to forgive the person that did that to me.*" Now with this statement you are indicating that you're looking at the whole business of forgiving from a mistaken place. You are looking at it as though forgiving is *for the other person*. If you forgive that person, he/she will feel better.

As we've seen, that is simply wrong. Not the bit about that person feeling better - they might, or they might not, but the issue here is YOU. You're the one who needs to feel better because of what was done to you. The other person has to take care of their own matters. You're not responsible for making them feel better, *but you are responsible for making yourself feel better*.

And that is where forgiving comes into the picture. You see, forgiving is *for you*. If you forgive a person who has done you a wrong, something that hurt you, *you are the one who will reap the benefit*. The energy that connects you to the bad thing, action, event, will have been switched off in the process of forgiving. So when thoughts about the event come up again, your inner state of being will no longer react in fury, pain, or despair, but will - in time - become totally neutral about it. Admittedly, this is not an immediate process. Forgiving is something that takes place over time, and not from one moment to the next, but forgiving has to do with your *intention to forgive*, and then, each time thoughts about what was done to you arise, you once again affirm to yourself that your intention is to forgive in order to become free, and because you love yourself enough to do this.

Do you have any idea what the negative inside of you does to you, and how little you can afford not to finish unfinished business?

It can affect your physical health, creating such problems as high blood pressure, unhealthy cholesterol levels, stress, accelerated heart rate, all of which can eventually lead you to diseases of many kinds.

So the negative inside of you is something you need to get a handle on. More than anything, it would be very helpful if you could begin to realize *that you literally cannot afford the luxury of having any unfinished business in your life. In order to start the process of eliminating it from your life, you need to become aware of how much it pulls you into the past. By pulling you into the past, it pulls you back into the low energy associated with the negativity of whatever the unfinished business is.*

What does unfinished business look like? Unfinished business is typically one or more of the following:

- anger
- resentment
- hurt
- guilt
- shame
- anxiety
- rage
- depression

What is the quickest way to deal with it? *Forgiving.* This three-pronged quote from a section about this topic in *Rewiring the Soul* puts it succinctly:

- Recognize that not forgiving holds parts of you in the past.
- Understand that forgiving does not mean you condone what was done, nor does it mean you now need to have a wonderful relationship with that person - you may need to

move on, but by forgiving, the hold that the event had over you, will be gone.

- Forgiving also does not mean forgetting – but it does mean, removing the charge from the memory.

Forgive the past and it will no long own you. Forgive and you will be free. Forgive and the love you have for yourself will have won over any of your feelings of anger, pain and resentment. And loving yourself is your greatest connection to your soul.

Chapter Eight

Paths to Loving the Self

The highest, most decisive experience is to be alone with one's
own self. You must be alone to find out what supports you, when
you find that you cannot support yourself. Only this experience
can give you an indestructible foundation.
Carl Gustav Jung

We have stringent habits of hygiene for our bodies, teeth
and hair. We spend much time ensuring our outer aspect looks and
smells good before we hit the road. We spend exorbitant amounts
of money on the latest fashion - not only to look good - but also to
look as though we belong (i.e., fashionable). And so we *decorate*
ourselves on the outside.

Do you see how ludicrous that is? Oh, I don't mean that it's
ludicrous or wrong to be clean and dress well, but that it's ludicrous
that we start our decorating process from the outside, as opposed

to from the inside. But that takes us right back to our mass media and the way we have been socialized - even by well-meaning parents who might not be labeled superficial at all.

We want our lives to be filled with peace and harmony, but we only spend a fraction, if any, of the time that we spend on that outer decorating process as compared to the time we spend on the inner one. Decorating yourself from the inside out literally means that the *intention to work magic on the inside* must be strong, and that this intention translates into time and consistency spent on that inner decoration.

How does your house come to be as beautiful as it is? Probably one of the reasons derives from the amount of time and love you have devoted to it, even if you did it on a shoestring budget and went from garage sale to flea market in order to source beautiful pieces that you then patiently and lovingly restored. Devotion, love and time are elements that you also require for the inner process. You simply would not expect your hair, your clothes, your face, your body, etc. to look good without some effort, and so you also *can not expect your inner self to shine* without time, love and devotion.

Think of your inner Self as the part of you that will never grow old, as the part of you that will always be. Doesn't it make more sense to spend *at least as much* love, time and devotion on decorating that eternal part of yourself, as you do on the outer part? *Isn't that who you really are?* Or do you actually believe that you are the wrinkles (or perhaps no wrinkles yet) on your face, or the designer label of clothing you wear? And if that inner part is who you really are, then that part of you deserves attention, time, devotion and love. Care for it at least as much as you care for the state of your skin, muscles, hair or nails. Grow it, decorate it, and care for it every single day of your life. Having a good hair day is great. Having a good life of inner peace, joy, harmony and freedom is priceless. In the following sections of this chapter we'll examine some of the paths that can take you there.

Being Conscious

The sooner you realize that the best way to live your life is by truly becoming acquainted with yourself, the sooner you will have crossed one of the biggest hurdles in life. Why are you here? To become important and surround yourself with important people and to acquire many things? To worry about remaining young and beautiful? To *be more* or to *know more* or to *have more* than other people you know?

> My own understanding is the sole treasure I possess, and the greatest. Though infinitely small and fragile in comparison with the powers of darkness, it is still a light, my only light.
> Carl Gustav Jung

Or could it be that while some of the above is certainly valid, the real reason you are here, in fact, goes far beyond that? Perhaps it has much more to do with the possibility that you are here to learn - as Seth would have put it - about *the eternal validity of your soul?* If so, then doesn't it make sense that you need to get to know yourself? And that means that in a sense you would be coming home; coming home to your *true* Self, to your soul. Such a process of becoming conscious also signifies that you come closer to loving yourself because all steps towards the core, towards the soul, are inter-related and they all lead all of us closer to that which we may truly be. Famed philosopher and Jesuit Pierre Teilhard de Chardin wrote that we are not human beings having a spiritual experience. We are *spiritual beings having a human experience.*

At a gathering of social acquaintances, you may have noticed how simple it is to become aware of others' failings. This one goes on and on. That one has garlicky breath. Another one always talks about his/her health. A fourth keeps looking over your shoulder to see if someone more important than you has arrived. Another clings to you in fear of standing alone, a sixth invariably pulls out photos of the children, and that one over there, that you're trying to avoid, all too often tells you what your political opinions ought to be.

Not a big deal, you might say, and it certainly is not. But what *is* a big deal, is that in all of this you have not seen your *own*. You are still completely *blind* to your own shortcomings, I mean. You remain blind to the only one that you can - in fact - do something about: you. But in order to do so, in order to bring about changes within yourself, you'll need to cast that eagle eye towards yourself instead of outward. This requires becoming conscious and aware. The Dalai Lama said: *To be aware of a single shortcoming in oneself is more useful than to be aware of a thousand in someone else.*

It's more useful and it's also much harder. The truthful look at the self - on the path towards finding the connection to your inner core, your soul - is always much more difficult, than the look outside, at all those others in your life. But if you do it - if you take that look at the self - you need to learn how to do it with love. Likewise, remember to keep loving the self in mind at all times because when mistakes happen, when you believe you have failed, recognize that - as Richard Bach put it - they can all just be called *unexpected learning experiences.*

This works as long as you let it. In other words, if you make a mistake and fall into despair, and believe you will never get over it, or convince others that you are actually capable and intelligent and not what you showed yourself to be during the making of the mistake, then obviously you'll find it much harder to make a learning experience of your mistake.

But if you open yourself to this - to the fact that all mistakes can lead to learning - and to realizing that if a toddler had not fallen the number of times he did, he would never have learned to walk (and we certainly don't call *that* process a mistake), or again, if a child learning how to speak, or particularly a child learning how to speak several languages all at the same time, makes mistakes, or uses the correct word but in the wrong language, no one considers that a mistake either. Quite the contrary, we admire it, we comment on how intelligent the child is to be able to speak in more than one language. One of the reasons we do this, is because we love and approve of the child. Learning to love and approve of yourself in similar fashion is, as stated, both an elementary and central part of becoming conscious.

Let's learn to look at our own mistakes the same way. Let's use them to our advantage. Let's learn from these unexpected learning experiences.

But being conscious is not only about being aware of the self and all we do, and how we react at all times, how we feel, what we say, and so on, it's also about continually being aware that one of the reasons you are here is because on some level of your *Self* you wish and want to grow exponentially in such a way that your inner light expands.

Look at it like this: You take occasional walks for your health. Then you start doing it on a daily basis. One day you decide to rev it up a notch and become a power walker. After months of increasing your speed and perhaps the amount of time you dedicate to this, you start running. At first you only run for a few minutes and then walk again, alternating between the two until you become stronger, and your lung capacity increases. And you find, after a time, that you are able to run, perhaps at first only for one or two kilometers, but then you can do more and greater distances. And so you decide to train for a marathon. And eventually you run your first one.

Why would you imagine that it is any different with increasing and expanding your own inner light? The light that is in you can grow, but it grows best if you work with what you already have. C.S. Lewis, magical, mystical author of many books, among others the beloved *Narnia Chronicles* that opened such a profusion of delightful doors in my childhood brain, but also respected theologian, wrote: *To act on the light one has is almost the only way to more light.*

Becoming Self-Aware

One of the things you do when you start becoming aware of the self, is to become aware of your appearance. I'm not talking so much about your physical appearance - although that is, of course, part of it - as about your *inner* appearance. Perhaps you feel you missed out on love as a child, and so you find it difficult to see your own beauty. Perhaps ever since then, your life hasn't been easy, and so - even more *now* - you find it difficult to see your own beauty. Or perhaps someone in your early life was very focused on outer, physical beauty, and you - in their eyes - just didn't measure up. However it went, you now have problems with this topic of seeing your own beauty.

What often happens is that you tend to believe that you first need someone else to *see* it before you can see it yourself. But then, when someone else at some point in your life does talk to you about your own beauty, you realize that you also have great difficulty believing them, or even if you do believe in their honesty on some level - you are incapable of internalizing it, and so for you, it just isn't so, and you continue to not see your own beauty.

Here's what lies at the crux of the above scenario: if you have not learned to *love yourself*, it makes little difference how many others tell you that you are beautiful, stunning, amazing, incredible, gifted, etc., because you just won't take it on board in a way that is important. If you have trouble believing me, just think of the wonderfully gifted and beautiful people in the world who distance themselves from their inner demons by abusing alcohol and drugs, or who have even taken that final step of a desperate life and committed suicide.

So: loving yourself. That's what lies at the bottom of it all. And if you did not learn this as a child, due to altogether frequent dysfunctional homes (it doesn't have to be abusive to be dysfunctional; a workaholic father, or a mother too wrapped up in her social life is enough, or simply parents who never learned how to communicate on levels that go beyond *how was your day*, and *the mortgage payment has gone up* and *what's for dinner*), so if you didn't learn to love yourself as a child, *you have to learn it now*!

It took me a long time not to judge myself
through someone else's eyes.
Sally Field

How?

- Make a priority of yourself in healthy ways.
- Work on your inner well-being consistently, realizing that without it, you have little chance of seeing your own beauty.
- Recognize that by taking baby steps in this direction, you are consistently sending conscious and subconscious messages to yourself each time you do it, that you are working on loving yourself.

Becoming aware of the self in this process of loving the self entails much more, or course, and you will find more material in Chapters 2 and 9. The subject was also discussed in both of my previous books in detail. But here are some of the most important aspects to bear in mind:

- Use a strategy of any kind to remember to be aware (one very simple one is to put up some post-it's in your house and office - on the mirror, the laptop screen, the fridge, etc., and to write on them 'what am I thinking?' or 'what am I feeling?'. You don't need to do this for a long time - just long enough to make it a habit, so that you will, indeed remain aware at all times).

- Take the *mindfulness walk* once a day (see Appendix B). Remember: it's only 15 minutes. It will help you begin to become aware of how often during the course of your day your thoughts take charge of you. When that happens, you are not aware and certainly not in charge of how you feel. That - putting it bluntly - is a highly unhealthy way to live, but quite simple to change. Practiced diligently, the mindfulness walk will take you a long way towards the goal of being in charge of those thoughts and the feelings they bring up in you.

- Practice the brief *gratitude exercise* (see Appendix A, and also see the section on the subject later in this chapter) at *any* time and in *any* situation during your day when you feel that you need a brief inner respite. It will help you process difficult thoughts and feelings in order to momentarily bring you to a place of inner balance and equanimity. What you're looking to achieve is a state of inner well-being, or at least, as said, inner balance, *no matter what the circumstances*. This requires remaining aware of yourself and your state. It also requires recognizing that being in charge of this is your own responsibility, and that the sooner you take on this responsibility, the sooner you will find yourself living a life of freedom as opposed to one where you depend on others for your inner well-being and happiness.

- Finally, in this process of becoming aware of the self, you will notice that your *inner* appearance becomes more and more important to you: are you judgemental? Critical? Do you gossip? Are you impatient? Unkind? Lacking in compassion? These and other questions will begin to clamor for attention within you and you will notice that as you attend to their demands of improvement, you increase your love for yourself and you see your own beauty and light to an ever-growing degree.

Assuming Responsibility for the Self

Self-responsibility in the way I'm discussing it in this book as we have seen, refers to being responsible for all that you think, feel, say and do, as well as how you react to everything that happens. It also includes the body, because what is all the above, if we're not ensuring that this body that houses us, is also functioning as immaculately as we are striving for all those other elements of our integral self to be?

Many years ago one of Stuart Wilde's wonderful *little* books fell into my hands, one of which is *still*, after over a quarter of a century, on my bedside table. At any rate, in the one I read (not the night table one), he mentions waking up, having some nice green lettuce (or something like that) for breakfast, and then going out for a jog.

In the naiveté of my youth, I remember being hugely amused - and repelled - by such a bizarre notion and I certainly had no intention of emulating the author. Now, in the wisdom of my years, while I still don't tend to have lettuce for breakfast, I certainly have a number of habits, nutritional and otherwise, that others might find bizarre - or at least amusing.

> There is overwhelming evidence that the higher the level of self-esteem, the more likely one will treat others with respect, kindness, and generosity. People who do not experience self-love have little or no capacity to love others.
> Nathaniel Branden

But what has happened throughout these years? I learned to respect *and care and be responsible for* this very special *house* of mine. I want it to be efficient and useful for a good many decades to come. I want it to provide me with optimal functioning at all times, to allow me to live not only with the energy I have to do all the things I constantly am inventing to do, but also with the vitality I feel inside of me, and the speed with which my brain functions when faced with *out-of-the-box* thinking, or cutting edge research that causes all my previous paradigms to tumble off of their shelves.

I want the excitement I am capable of feeling every day to endure all the days of my life. I want to be able to fill my lungs with fresh air right down to the very bottom without coughing or feeling pressure in my chest. I want to be able to stretch and twist and turn and walk and exercise without pain or breathlessness. In a word, I want to be as healthy as I possibly can until the last possible moment. And then I'll be quite thrilled to go on to the next adventure.

So guess who has the responsibility for that? And guess who has to make choices about that responsibility every day, all day long? About what I eat, what I drink, how often I exercise, and so on. Obviously what works for me may not work for you and vice versa, and there are many roads that lead to Rome, but clearly, you don't have to be a rocket scientist in order to recognize that you need to make this a priority in your life - if you are interested in living in an optimally functioning *house.*

Now let's have a look at the responsibility for loving yourself. As I've repeated over and over in this book, loving yourself lies at the beginning of all roads that lead you to inner peace, joy, harmony, and freedom. The underpinnings for finding balance and harmony in your life rest on you being able to love yourself. If you do not love yourself, or at least begin the process of loving yourself, most of everything else you do in the arena of personal transformation will not bring you the desired results.

But – as so much else in the personal development field – it's easier said than done. Loving yourself is so much more than indulging in some long denied desire, or lying in a bubble bath surrounded by scented candles while relaxing music soothes your jagged edges.

Loving yourself begins first and foremost with the recognition that if you are not in a place of well-being inside yourself, *it's up to you to do something about it.* That should become your priority. Imagine you are the parent of a small child. Your child is upset, or sad, or angry or frightened. You as the loving parent, would attempt to soothe your child. You might embrace her, talk about what is going on, or do any number of things designed to help your child view the situation with new eyes in order to find some measure of inner harmony and peace about whatever has transpired.

But in order for this to happen you would *need to be closely connected to your child,* you would *need to have strong communication with your child,* and you would *need to be totally aware of your child's feelings.* Furthermore, you'd *need to want to be there* for your child.

Clearly this is a simple analogy about how you need to be dealing with yourself and why: in order to show yourself that you love yourself (because that's how it starts), you must be aware of yourself and your feelings at all times and be conscious or aware enough to *choose* to do something about them at all times, in order to bring yourself to an inner state of well-being.

Does that mean that you would never allow yourself to feel pain or sorrow or worry or have any other type of negative feeling? Does it mean you would keep yourself in some iron grip of control so that you would not have those feelings? *Absolutely not!* But it *does* mean that you would be willing to choose to first allow yourself to find a place of inner balance, harmony, or equanimity *before* focusing on the above-described feelings and deciding how to deal with them from the vantage point of this new inner position.

What would you do if you find yourself worrying about your health or money or your relationship? You would recognize that worrying takes you absolutely nowhere, you would recognize that it is much more proactive to do your due diligence about whatever it is that is going on in your life (attempt to resolve it by giving it a certain amount of time per day – *but only that amount of time* - in your life, brainstorming, consulting, researching about the situation), and you would then *choose to focus on something else in order to help yourself move to a better place inside,* because that is what you do for those that you love. And as you begin to do that for yourself, over and over again, you begin to realize that you are on the road to loving yourself.

What would you do if someone has just made you incredibly angry? Or how would you deal with someone who is playing the role of energy vampire in your life, or being emotionally unavailable with you? Remember, that part of this process has to do with you becoming aware of yourself, and taking responsibility for yourself and how you react to situations and people.

So that means that if you are taking responsibility for yourself because you have become more aware of yourself, you will also have begun to accept the fact that you are ultimately responsible for everything you think, feel, say and do, as well as taking responsibility for how you react at all times, *no matter what the outer circumstances*. Hence, when at first glance it appears that someone else has made you angry, i.e., that it is their fault that you are angry, you begin to see that you have a choice about how you feel at that particular moment. You realize you *can choose how you react*. And if you consciously choose to continue to have a reasonably good day despite another person's near negative effect on the state of your being, you are beginning to show yourself that you love yourself enough in order to do this.

In each of us there is another whom we do not know.
Carl Gustav Jung

A much more extreme example is a poor - or even terminal - health diagnosis. *What do you do with your state of being under such circumstances?* The simple answer is: *exactly the same.* The harder answer is that of course in order for you to do that, you will have already had to practice this in less traumatic situations. (Think: how do we become good drivers whose reflexes are finely honed so that in the split second prior to an accident, you are capable of reacting in such a way that you avoid the accident). Clearly, you would not be capable of dealing with your inner state in the way described, if you were trying to do it the first time on the day of the health diagnosis, in the same way a weight lifter at the gym would not be able to tackle the heavier barbells until many hours and days and months of practice had taken place.

At first glance it may appear that these suggestions are small and you may be asking if that's all there's to it. In effect, *that is all there's to it*, but it is the continual practice of a lifetime to perfect this. If you start today, right now, this evening you will already feel better about how you are dealing with yourself. You'll recognize that you've taken some steps to love yourself. And a part of you will feel just as loved as the child who has been enveloped in the loving arms of a caring and emotionally generous *adult* parent. This will bring you ever closer to inner peace and freedom, and this will bring you joy.

Note: merely following the suggestions in this section of this chapter and doing the Mindfulness Walk described in Appendix B - on a daily basis - will take you a long way towards the goal of loving yourself.

Serving Both the Inner & Outer Self

A person who had been working very consciously and diligently on re-shaping the inner world, once said to me: *I feel so excited when I do this,* and my reply was: *it's because for the first time you are truly coming into connection with yourself.*

There is always an inner sensation of resonance and excitement when in some fashion you connect with your *true* Self, your *inner* Self, or, as many authors have put it: *your soul.* You feel energized, you feel good, there is, in fact, a similar sensation to how you feel when the one you love enters the room and you catch a glimpse of him/her in the distance. There is a simple reason for this:

as you come into contact with yourself, you also begin the process of learning to love the Self and quite frankly, there is nothing quite as magnificent as that. Loving the self is the basis for so much if you seek inner peace, harmony, joy and well-being, that to not begin to do it consciously, if at all possible, is to deny yourself the greatest of tools for health and well-being in all dimensions.

> When there is no enemy within, the enemies
> outside cannot hurt you.
> African Proverb

Once you are conversant with that sensation of excitement that arises as you begin to connect with your inner Self, you will also begin to understand what lies behind the *pull of what you really love.* There is a similar feeling of excitement when you begin to connect (work, study, hobby) with something that you really love. And of course the reason is based on the same principle: the excitement you feel when you *do* that thing (whatever it is), or even just *think* about doing that thing, comes about because you are connecting to some core element of that *true* Self, that *inner* Self, or your *soul*, that was referred to above.

So the pull of what you really love is much stronger than any other pull - stronger than the pull of desire for material acquisition, stronger than the desire for social, professional or academic prominence, and when you feel that pull, you would be well advised to heed it. It was Rumi who said: *Let yourself be silently drawn by the stronger pull of what you really love.* He also said, and this quote always brings me a sensation of great joy: *When you do things from your soul, you feel a river moving in you, a joy.*

And what you really love also encompasses so many other factors. How much loving is there in your life? Is it palpable on a daily basis? When loving becomes second nature, you can truly state that your life is filled with loving. And by loving I mean all the variations of love we know:

- love for children
- love for parents
- love for partners
- love for friends
- love for yourself
- love for beauty
- love for the vicarious thrill of doing whatever you enjoy most
- love for awe-inspiring dawns and spectacular sunsets
- love for refreshing rain and silent snowfall
- love for brilliant sunshine and love for velvet nights
- but also love for *life* and *all those* who share it with you - we are *all one.*

The Buddha said: *Until he has unconditional and unbiased love for all beings, man will not find peace.* And Kahlil Gibran said: *Wake at dawn with a winged heart and give thanks for another day of loving.* As you choose to make every day another day of loving you foment within you the ability to love yourself. Love begets love, and even when circumstances are such that you do not feel you are receiving love in obvious ways from others (as might have been the case with Nelson Mandela those 27 long years while he was imprisoned on Robben Island, or Viktor Frankl while he was in Auschwitz), you can still choose to make your day a day of love. It is your inner disposition and inner self that sets the benchmark - not what is happening in the outer world.

How much of your life contains joy? How much joy do you emanate? How much joy do you *feel*? How much joy is available to you at any time? If your answer contains a heavy load of *it depends on my circumstances*, I would venture to reply that your circumstances do not - and *should not* - carry the responsibility for your joy or lack of it. If they do, you will never be free, because you understand that what is external to you cannot be in your power, or only occasionally, but what is internal to you can be, should be, and perhaps already is in your power. This means that you have accepted responsibility for your inner state of being at all times. This means you have opted to live an aware life, because without awareness you simply can't take on such responsibility.

Another aspect of this is that your joy may be contagious to others. Or at the very least, they may feel great desire to also be able to experience such joy. In effect, this means that ultimately your joy has the opportunity to create joy for others. This is such a gift. It was Mother Teresa who said: *joy is a net of love by which you can catch souls.* And you can decide to go catch yourself some souls today and every day. You do this with love, and you do it with joy, and the place from which you bring the love and the joy is from inside of yourself where you love yourself.

Most people have heard the story of the man who left his rather humble home in the village to go out into the world to seek riches, which I briefly referred to earlier in this book. In some versions he finds riches and in other versions he doesn't. But in all versions, when he finally returns home, he digs up the garden to plant corn, or he goes into the cellar to look for something, or he does a totally different thing which eventually leads him to the same situation as the garden or cellar version: he finds great riches that have been there all along in his own small and very humble home that he had left so many long years ago. Enormous wealth was there all along. He had simply never recognized it. He had not even been able to imagine it. And yet, all he had to do was look there as opposed to outside in the world.

We spend our lives looking for something, wanting something, and moving towards something. Whatever it is that we seek is always out there, tomorrow, next week, when I achieve this or that goal, or as soon as I lose ten pounds, go on that vacation, or receive the promotion. What we so often appear to ignore, to forget, or to totally overlook, is that what we really seek is almost always inside of us. *Not* the position, the money, the fame or the honor, but the way we imagine we would *feel* if we had it. That is what is inside of us.

The secret to understanding that is to recognize that loving yourself first, before looking for all the rest, *will* provide you with that feeling; *will* give you what you desire so fervently. Feeling good about yourself, feeling approved of (by yourself), feeling respected (by yourself), feeling esteemed (by yourself), and feeling loved (by yourself) is the jewel we *all* have inside, if only we will take the time and energy to look for it.

Numerous authors refer to this. George Moore says: *A man travels the world in search of what he needs and returns home to find it.* T.S. Eliot said it in *Little Giddings* from which I quoted earlier in this book. Rumi said: *It may be that the satisfaction I need depends on my going away, so that when I've gone and come back, I'll find it at home.* My greatest desire for you - and my reason for writing this book - is that you begin walking down the road to loving yourself.

In some fashion we can all apply this to our own lives. We may or may not have found success and riches in the outer world, but when we begin to scratch at the surface of our own being, of our own Self, and when we begin to connect with our own soul, we begin to fathom the magnitude of riches inherent in the Self - riches that are not immediately visible to the naked eye, but they are rapidly visible to the inner eye and inner knowing. In the connection to the Self you see the treasure, and you recognize that the treasure you have sought out there lies in you because it is you - the eternal you.

This is what the person I referred to at the beginning of this section meant with the words: *I feel so excited when I do this*. The connection to the inner Self had been established and therefore an inner spark was ignited. As said, it's the same thing when people are on the verge of discovering their own purpose or meaning in life (whatever it may be): there tends to be an inner excitement, butterflies in the solar plexus, perhaps even a breathlessness, because - again - the connection to the inner self is being mobilized.

A good part of this inner connection to the Self has to do with praising the self, although praising the self, as we saw, tends to have a bad reputation. It smacks - or so insist many - of pride, egotism, perhaps even selfishness. And so we often learn, as we have seen, and possibly at a very young age, to abstain from praising the self. Or if we do, we feel guilty. And of course if we don't praise the self, how can we possibly *love the self*?

> When an inner situation is not made conscious
> it appears as fate outside.
> Carl Gustav Jung

Let's focus for a moment on a young couple. Their 11-month-old baby is just barely beginning to attempt the move from his hands and knees to his pudgy little legs. He grabs on to the furniture, to his mother's dress, to his father's trousers, all in an attempt to raise himself to his feet. And what happens? He is given *praise*. His parents are beside themselves with pride and joy about his accomplishment. The baby *feels good* about himself. And in part because of all the applause and the inner feeling of confidence that comes with it, as well as with his own inner feeling good about himself, he soon succeeds in his endeavor and before you know it, he's running, then he's on a tricycle, and then on a bike off to school.

It's a simple analogy (and I hope you can forgive the fact that I make use of this scenario frequently in this book), but it's something for you to consider deeply. Praising the self is *not* selfish, nor is it about an unhealthy or bad pride. Praising the self comes from love of the Self. Love of the Self is deeply intertwined with connecting to the Self - both the inner and outer self. Love of the Self is *not* something undesirable or inappropriate that should be eradicated from your character. Quite the contrary: love of the Self is one of the most, if not *the* most life-giving and health-supporting thing you can do for yourself, and by extension, for all others. *Be the change you wish to see in the world* Gandhi said.

So go ahead: look at your past and make a list of all those things you have done that make you proud. Perhaps not something that will appear in the *Wall Street Journal*, or even the local paper. But things that have given you pride in yourself and that have caused you to like and love that *one* that you are just a bit more. Look at that list often. *It is so infinitely more important to examine the list at length than it is to examine your problems.* Healthy self-love and pride of self are furthermore the gateways to compassion, connection with, and love for all others.

Find something to be proud about today and every day. And find something to love about yourself not just today but every day.

Recognizing There is Always a Choice

Growing into adulthood in our modern society, most of us, particularly in our western civilization, have taken on much of the murkiness that pervades life in general. It has come to take up residence, so to speak, within us. The elements that we are all so familiar with: greed, anger, spite, competitiveness that goes to any lengths to win, self-righteousness, lies, arrogance, entitlement, and sloth, to mention only a few, form a major part of this. And prior to that societal murkiness, perhaps we had already taken on the dark dysfunctionality of our own family.

Nobody can make you feel inferior without your consent.
Eleanor Roosevelt

Societal murkiness and dark dysfunctionality make for a muddiness inside, a lack of light and clarity, a lack of peace and harmony, and clearly, no real hope for freedom from these constrictions.

One of the symbolic meanings of the lotus is that just as the flower emerges from the mud, so too can you *choose* - if you have grown to love yourself - to take a path that will lead you out of the dark mud, mire, and morass to the *state of the lotus within*, a state of enlightenment. And although I borrow the word from spiritual literature, I use it here in a more practical sense.

Allow that inner Self to emerge from the murkiness and dark by becoming conscious of the fact that such a process lies in your hands. Take on responsibility for yourself and your growth, responsibility for your inner freedom, joy and harmony. Choose to do this from a position of conscious awareness that there are always choices to be made, and *absolutely each choice* leads to a different set of consequences.

And therefore it is obvious that if you want your future to be different you will need to make different choices because you want different circumstances than your present ones. So what do you have to change in order to ensure that different future?

Here's a very simple answer: You will need to consider changing as many of your current *now moments* as possible. This will bring a process into motion that will bring about different now moments in your future. Here are some examples:

- When you wake up and see a grey sky and think *oh, no, not another grey day - I hate grey weather*, you need to be aware of those thoughts and what they do to your energy, and then change that and think other thoughts that bring about another kind of inner feeling than the *oh no* one.

- When you drive to work and get impatient at traffic and clumsy or careless drivers around you, you need to be aware of what that impatience does to your inner energy and change that and work on becoming more patient, and perhaps simultaneously work on not focusing on the traffic and its frustration, but use your down time in the car in order to listen to inspiring or motivational CD's. (Also see the section titled 'Collect' in Chapter 4, as well as a sample listing in Appendix D).

- When you put off doing something today, telling yourself that you can do it tomorrow, you may wish to reconsider, and decide not to put it off, in order to not only feel better about yourself due to having set procrastination to one side, but also, in order to have a clearer, less cluttered day tomorrow.

- When you react to your spouse, parent, child, sibling, or business partner in a blind way, not thinking about how you are reacting, but simply reacting *from the gut, reactively, blindly,* you may wish to reconsider and start practicing to really become more aware in order to have *conscious*, as opposed to *blind* reactions. This will set off a chain reaction, the beneficial consequences of which you can only imagine.

- When you decide what to put into your mouth, you may wish to change some of that, once you give a second of thought to the effect of that food on your body and mind.

- When you decide what to put into your mind via books, magazines, movies, music, conversations, people you socialize with, etc., you may wish to change some of that.

- When you feel stressed or pained about something, and it goes on and on in your mind, and you *just know* that there is nothing you can do about it, or you know that it is continually in your mind because of what was done to you, thinking: *how could I not think otherwise about such pain?*, you may wish to reconsider and start using awareness to do something about the direction into which your thoughts go.

Any or all of these examples will serve to make your future different. Your choices are the decisive factor.

Now let's examine what you do with your habits. Certainly you only rarely choose them with care. Generally speaking, your habits are formed long before you think about them consciously (if ever) and so you continue with them without considering whether they *embellish* you or not. What do are habits that embellish? Simply that by having and maintaining such habits, they serve you well, as opposed to blindly leading you to places you might prefer not to frequent. Consider these examples:

- A habit of having bread with every meal may cause the pounds to creep up on you and before you know it, you find yourself in a place where it is very difficult to stop the habit, and yet if you continue with it, you will need a new wardrobe (to say the least).

- A habit of not listening when others speak to you because you are busy thinking about your answer, may cause you to do less well than you would like in your professional environment and in your personal sphere may eventually cause you to lose your partner or spouse.

- A habit of watching three hours of television every evening may have numerous results including unwanted weight piling up due to being such a couch potato, and brain cells losing their strength due to not being used, other than in this passive way.

- A habit of judging others (even if only in your mind), may cause you to never see the real person behind whatever it is that you are judging.

- A habit of blaming others for whatever you are unable to do perfectly yourself may cause you to never learn to take responsibility for yourself.

- A habit of giving in to others' manipulations may cause you to lead a life filled with bitterness and resentment due to never learning to say no and continuing with those unhealthy boundaries.

- A habit of continually demanding perfection from yourself may cause you to live a deeply unhappy life because you will find it nearly impossible to live up to those unattainable standards that you have set for yourself *because you do not love yourself* in healthy ways that would allow you to accept yourself as you grow towards goals as opposed to demanding achievement of those goals *now*.

Your habits determine - to a large degree - the quality of your life. Your habits also speak of how much you love yourself. Greater self-love brings better habits with it automatically. *Choose them well*, and if - when they were formed - you were not yet aware enough to choose, now, that you are more aware, take them under a microscope, examine them, and begin to discard those that do not serve your highest good.

And of course just as your habits influence your life, so does having the inner wherewithal to choose your attitude at all times become a recipe for well-being. If you know that no matter what the circumstances, you will be capable of choosing an attitude that maintains your own inner well-being or balance, you know that nothing - but absolutely nothing - that comes your way will have the ability to throw you.

As we've seen, most people can't do this. The main reason is because only few in our culture talk about this way of living when we are growing up. And then, of course, once we *have* grown up, we're convinced that it is otherwise. In other words, we're convinced that our attitude is determined by our circumstances and that we have little or no choice about it. If things are going well, we are happy. If they are not, we are most definitely not happy. And that's it.

But there are those others, over the millennia, that have propagated another kind of thinking. Not everyone is aware of them, not everyone has paid attention to them, but they are out there and have been out there for those whose eyes are open since the beginning of time. Here is their message: being conscious and aware of yourself at all times, as well as accepting responsibility for yourself and your inner state at all times, allows you to choose your attitude in the face of any kind of situation at all.

You'll need to have a brief dialogue with yourself if you wish this to take root in your life. The brief dialogue needs to be held when a situation falls into your life that would normally render you unhappy, fearful, stressed, frustrated, angry, impatient, critical, judgmental, or self-aggrandizing. Add to that list any other you like that lies on the negative side of the emotional continuum we are all subject to, and then realize that whether or not you go in that direction will from now on depend entirely on you and not on your circumstances, if you practice it. The dialogue might go like this:

- Such-and-such has happened.
- This normally makes me feel unhappy or causes me to have this (negative) _____ attitude.
- But I have a choice about how I feel.
- Do I wish to feel unhappy or have this (negative) _____ attitude about it?
- No I don't.
- So if I have a choice, what might be a better attitude or feeling to have?
- I could *choose* to remain calm.
- I could *choose* to find a place of inner balance before I decide what to do.
- I could *choose* to look at this as a learning experience.

There are many variations on this theme, but they all come down to one common denominator: *it is up to you. It is your choice.* And that is how simple it is. Obviously it requires practice - but then so do most things that are worthwhile attaining. Viktor Frankl said: *the last of human freedoms is to choose one's attitude in any given set of circumstances.* Frankl came to recognize this during his years at Auschwitz.

Beauty, Gratitude & Mindfulness

Imagine having gone through a bad divorce, financially and regarding child custody. It happened a while ago and basically no longer bothers you. But today you caught yourself thinking about it and remembering how you got royally messed about.

Or imagine that you didn't get a promotion at some point in your life when you should have, because a colleague essentially stepped on your shoulders and got what you should have received. In the meantime you have become successful, and this really no longer irritates you, but today you caught yourself thinking about it and reviewing how you were the recipient of such unfair treatment from management.

Or imagine that you had written a very clever essay in your English Literature class, you got top grades for it, but when it came time to read a portion of one of the essays to the class, your professor chose to read that of another student whose grade was lower than yours. You were hurt at the time, but it's over, and you certainly have other things on your mind, but today you caught yourself thinking about that long-ago event, and remembering how it dismayed you.

And the time your girlfriend cheated on you. You were devastated, but now you have a new girl friend that you love in other, much more wonderful ways, and you are happy with her, but something triggered the memory of the infidelity, and so you feel the flood of obsession and betrayal all over again.

And as you find yourself in any of the above − or other similar − situations, you find that you spiral downwards into an inner state that is not good.

Your problem is you're too busy holding onto your unworthiness.
Ram Dass

It's of utmost importance to recognize what is going on here. The thoughts you are having about the event in question are *low-frequency thoughts* that literally erode the quality and the happiness and joy, the "now-ness" of your life. These are thoughts that immediately bring you to another state than the one you were previously on. If we could equate your state of being to a number on a scale of 0-10, where 0 is awful and 10 is superlative, you might have been going about your day at a 6, and when these thoughts occurred you spiraled down to a 4 or a 3 or even less.

What can you do about this? How can you control such thoughts?

As we've come to see, it is literally impossible to be the policeman of all your thoughts all of the time. But it is quite simple to be the observer of your state of being at all times. As you slide down to a lower frequency because of the type of thought described above, you will feel that your state of being has eroded, and gone down. You can do something about this. It's all up to you.

Become aware of yourself, your state of being, your feelings, and then make the choice to take action in order to bring yourself back up to another level by taking responsibility for yourself. Using gratitude is one of the most accessible ways of doing this.

A multitude of scientific studies all give the same results: feeling and focusing on gratitude is highly beneficial for your physiological, psychological, emotional and spiritual health. More and more of these studies are being funded since this information first hit the airwaves in the late 1990's and in an article I referred to what were at that time (2006) recent studies, indicating that *amazingly, the most important component to maintaining and/or raising our level of happiness is accomplished by keeping a gratitude journal.*

Whether you keep a journal, or practice the brief exercise in Appendix A, I'd like to encourage you to contemplate ten excellent reasons that demonstrate exactly why you should make gratitude an integral component of your daily routine, not something to do occasionally, or when you wake up, or when you go to bed, but to integrate it into your daily life in such a way that *it is always there – in your conscious awareness - in some fashion,* just as your awareness of the amount of light where you are is always present. It can easily (and painlessly) become second nature, if only you choose for gratitude to occupy that place in your life. And as you will soon see, adding a practice of gratitude (also see Appendix A) to your life automatically brings beauty and mindfulness into focus, and eventually that leads you to peace.

1. **Gratitude lowers your stress levels as measured by blood pressure and perspiration and breathing.**

    Because you focus on something that gives you a certain amount of happiness or pleasure, gratitude is capable of affecting you on these very physiological levels. If you think for a moment of a grinding problem in your life and note how it makes you feel, and then switch your focus to something beautiful in your surroundings, allowing yourself to feel gratitude for it being there (the blue sky, a flock of birds joyously lifting up from the trees in perfect formation to fly elsewhere, a frolicking puppy, a bold purple bougainvillea climbing up a white-washed garden wall, a contagiously laughing child behind a wrought-iron gate, the elusive scent of a night jasmine, the full moon in a star-lit sky, the burst of flavor in your mouth as you bite into a ripe peach, etc.), you will notice that you immediately begin to feel very different compared to how you felt a moment ago.

2. **Gratitude increases your levels of alertness, enthusiasm, determination, and attentiveness as indicated in several studies.**

    What happens when you think about a huge pile of work that needs to be done? Don't you feel a bit overwhelmed, perhaps even tired, just by thinking about it? Now quickly think about spending a two week vacation on Bora-Bora or traveling around a country you have yet to explore, perhaps Istanbul and the Cappadocia region of Turkey. Didn't you immediately feel more alert and enthused? It's exactly the same thing again with gratitude. As in the first point above, focus on something beautiful in your surroundings.

3. **Sleep duration and sleep quality are also positively affected by gratitude as indicated in the same studies.**
    We all know what happens to the quality of our sleep when we are worried and stressed. And what happens when our lives flow? When things are going well? Again, by focusing on gratitude, we get a similar effect, *even when things are not flowing.*

4. **By creating a good feeling inside of you, gratitude literally changes your energetic frequency.**
    It follows that if you change from a not-so-good feeling to a better one, your inner state of energy will increase, or quicken. Raising the energy of what you focus on, raises your energy in many different ways. Focus on a war movie with much devastation, grayness, desperation and mindless torture and killing, or focus on a movie such as *A Beautiful Mind* or *Eat, Pray, Love*, and you will clearly feel the energetic difference. Focusing on gratitude for something in your life, something as simple as the examples in the first point of this article, and you will immediately notice the change in energy.

5. **Gratitude allows you to shift your perspective about the matters you had been contemplating prior to feeling the gratitude.**
    When you change your inner energy, as established in the previous points, you will be in a new place inside your body,

mind, heart, and spirit. *This position in the new feeling and thinking place* will allow you to see whatever problem you are currently facing from a new perspective because when you feel better, you can see things differently. This may even allow you to more easily find a solution to your situation.

6. **Gratitude strengthens the neural pathway that demonstrates to you that you are capable of *choosing* to focus elsewhere whenever you wish.**

    As you focus on gratitude again and again, noticing the increase in energetic frequency, noticing that you *do feel better* by focusing on gratitude, you are not only creating a new habit and hence, creating and strengthening a new neural pathway to the detriment of earlier formed neural pathways that do not serve you well, but you are also creating the neural pathway of *belief in your own power to change your focus as and when you wish in order to benefit yourself.* And once you believe that changing how you feel is in your power and not in the power of your circumstances, you are embarked on the road towards inner peace and freedom.

7. **Gratitude strengthens another very important neural pathway that begins to determine that you *prefer* to be in this place of inner well-being that you achieve as you focus on gratitude, as opposed to the place you were in before you exercised your feelings of gratitude.**

    If you lived in a studio apartment as a student, and then started earning money and moved into a three bedroom home, you soon become habituated to more space. If you are accustomed to eating in fast food places and one day you start going to five star restaurants, you soon become habituated to a superior quality of food, surroundings and service. In the same way you rapidly become accustomed to being in a much better energetic state – a place of much greater inner well-being – once you begin to choose to focus on gratitude throughout your day. Being accustomed to being there, means that you will adjust back to being there quickly, on those occasions that you stray off the path energetically.

8. **By becoming a habit, gratitude automatically allows you to remain in a much better inner space that is not easily perturbed.**

    The stronger the habit, the more robust the neural pathway that is associated to your choice to focus on gratitude throughout your day. As this begins to become the *normal* place in which you live (i.e., a better place of inner well-being), your new *status quo*, it is much harder to perturb that place. In other words in the same way in which someone who trains at the gym on a regular basis, or someone who power walks or runs on a regular basis, has a physical condition that is harder to knock off kilter, so it also applies to someone who has chosen to have a continual feeling of inner well-being, and who will therefore not be easily thrown into a negative place *no matter what the outer circumstances.*

9. **Gratitude causes you to focus on the *now* as opposed to focusing on past pain or sorrow, or focusing on future worries.**

    Just for a moment think of something that is worrying you. For another moment think of something that caused you pain in the past. Now focus on something you are grateful for - perhaps the warmth of the sunshine flooding through your window, or the aroma of freshly baked bread coming from your kitchen, or the brilliance of the sun in the sky. Now evaluate: while you were focused on feeling gratitude, you no longer had the future worry or the past pain in your mind and emotions. The gratitude left no room for it – not if you allowed the gratitude to flood your being for that moment. And the reason for that, as we've clearly seen, is the fact that focusing on gratitude takes you – immediately – to the NOW where there is no room for thoughts and emotions from the past or future. It is a place of utter peace.

10. **Experiencing gratitude implies that your ego cannot dominate you because it can only dominate when you are not in the now.**

Using the term *ego* in the sense that it is that part of you that has untold unwanted thoughts that you feel you are not in control of, thoughts that in turn take you to untold feelings over which you also have no control, then by focusing on gratitude and bringing yourself into the now as explained in the previous point, your ego – all those unwanted thoughts and unwanted emotions brought about by those thoughts - no longer has the power to dominate you. *The one that you are when you are in the now* is the eternal you, the divine you, the you that always was and always will be and hence, the you that *is not the ego.*

Consider these points carefully. Incorporate them into your daily life. They are simple. They work. Your life improves. Your subconscious thought patterns and beliefs change. Your inner well-being increases and this new increased level of well-being becomes second nature. This - among so many other ways available to you - is how self-love begins to grow.

Chapter 9

What Changes? (And How to Get There)

What you think about yourself is much more important
than what others think of you.
Marcus Annaeus Seneca

Imagine having a blister that you don't take care of. It simply continues to hurt and chafe each time you wear the shoes that cause it. You may be able to fool yourself that it is gone, and yet, as soon as those shoes are on your feet, the skin gets red again, the blister re-develops, eventually it pops, causing even more discomfort, and then the chafing against the raw skin begins anew. Of course you may use a band aid, but by the next wearing you'll be in the same boat again. You may need to do something about those shoes - perhaps consider they were a mistake - get them stretched, or somehow manage to change how they and your heel interact. Once you do that, blisters will no longer form.

That is exactly what happens to the pain and chafing in your life when you begin to love the self. So much changes. So many things that were difficult before, or that hurt, or that sent you into paroxysms of panic and anxiety, simply no longer have the power to do so. Loving the self literally affects every aspect of your life. You feel a sense of empowerment that liberates you, because even when difficult or painful things occur, you feel so much more in control of your inner self and your reactions. This alone is enough to increase your inner well-being immeasurably.

> The moment you have in your heart this extraordinary thing called love and feel the depth, the delight, the ecstasy of it, you will discover that for you the world is transformed.
> Jiddu Krishnamurti

Loving the self changes - as we shall see throughout this chapter - your inner dialogue and how you self-soothe, your relationship to yourself, your relationship to your children (and because of *you*, their future relationship to their own children, because they will have grown up to be true adults, as opposed to most of us that did not), your relationship to your partner (including the way you love, your possible unhealthy boundaries, neediness, or emotional unavailability, among many others), your relationship to your life, and your concept of love, kindness and compassion in such a way that you are then able to truly comprehend that we are all one.

Your Inner Dialogue & How You Self-Soothe

The way you talk to yourself: the things you tell yourself, especially when something goes wrong, and the way in which you soothe yourself in large measure identify a fundamental aspect of what changes when you begin to love the self. Before loving yourself, your self-dialogue may be filled with dire thoughts, words, and images that create difficult-to-process feelings in you. *After* beginning to love yourself, you understand that part of loving yourself means that you have to engage in a radically different kind of conversation with yourself when outer circumstances spell trouble. By changing that inner dialogue, you are able to remain in (or bring yourself back to) a place of inner equilibrium, balance, peace, and harmony, and hence your reactions work *for* your well-being, *no matter what the outer circumstances*, as opposed to *against* your well-being.

Self-soothing is closely connected to this inner dialogue, because when something bad happens, what you tell yourself about it determines whether or not you'll be able to bring yourself to a place where you feel a measure of comfort, again, and I repeat: *no matter what the outer circumstances are.* How you self-soothe determines how well you're able to care for yourself during a moment of fear, panic, anxiety, pain, etc.

What does a child do when it falls and scrapes its knee, when it feels the pain and sees the blood? Typically it will wail, cry, or scream. A small child hasn't yet learned how to self-soothe in a healthy way. So someone else comes along (mother, father, an older sibling, grandmother, etc.) to pick up the child, hug it, give it a kiss and murmur soothing words. If the child never learns healthy self-soothing by the time he/she is a mid to older teen, as we have seen, alcohol, drugs, sex, etc., might form part of the 'caring' process when uncomfortable or painful emotions are being felt. That's obviously not healthy. And that is why caring for the self and loving the self offers such an unbridled opportunity to learn a manner of self-soothing that is good for you and that allows you to deal with whatever you are going through in a way that keeps you in balance and with a good amount of peace and harmony inside of you.

Imagine seeing one of your friends appear in a new Audi Spider that you've secretly coveted for years, another friend has dropped 10 pounds, seemingly and magically overnight, something that you've been trying to do unsuccessfully for such a long time, and yet another just landed a deal to expand his business that will net hundreds of thousands, if not more, over the next few years. You read about someone you've never even heard of who signed a record deal recently and now the hit single from the first CD has hit the charts not nationally, but globally - it went viral. Your best friend of many years never seems to stop being invited everywhere, another continually fills your ears with how wonderful life is, and a third can't stop talking about the children or grandchildren and how intelligent or successful or proactive they are. One of your acquaintances met a fascinating and charming widow/widower and is now getting married, the son of another friend was just promoted to Vice President of the company he works for, your golfing neighbor just started dating a stunning woman about 20 years younger than you, and of course the list *of all the good stuff that happens to others* goes on and on. And not only does it go on and on, but it's been happening that way ever since you can remember. *Always.*

> We delight in the beauty of the butterfly, but rarely admit
> the changes it has gone through to achieve that beauty.
> Maya Angelou

And although a part of you is happy (truly happy) for them, there is *another* part of you that is envious, or feels jealousy, depending on the situation. You're aware of it. You don't particularly like feeling envy or jealousy, but there it is, it pops up all the time when you hear of the good fortune that graces the lives of others. *These thoughts are the breeding-ground for your unhappiness.* The more they (the thoughts) occur, the more your habit of having those thoughts and hence your unhappiness grows. These are most definitely not thoughts of joy.

Here's what you can do: first, become aware (as you probably already are) that this is happening. Acknowledge that it does you no good. All the *bacteria* of those thoughts continually spread to infest you with discontent or unhappiness. Clearly, the thoughts must be tackled. Probably you are thinking that since they pop up unannounced and not because you 'will' them into being, there is little you can do about them. But there is, as we have seen throughout this book. *They have become a habit* that started years, perhaps even decades ago. And all you have to do is rid yourself of that habit, much as you might rid yourself of the habit of exploring a chipped corner of a tooth in your mouth with your tongue. At the beginning you would simply explore, but as time goes by, your tongue develops a very sore spot on the place where it hits the chipped tooth. It hurts. So now you pull back consciously each time your tongue wants to go there, and soon enough, your tongue stops doing it. You do this because you engage your conscious mind into stopping the process because of the pain it produces.

In the case of the thoughts of envy and jealousy that lead to unhappiness, *you do exactly the same thing*. As you hear of the wonderful thing that is happening to someone else, and you notice the thoughts of envy or jealousy arising, you have a short inner dialogue. You ask yourself whether you wish to pursue that thought. Probably the answer is no, because you are already aware of the fact that those thoughts only lead you to unhappiness. You may need to have a brief battle, because it may be that a part of you wishes to engage in the negative thought (what Eckhart Tolle would call the *pain body*), but you *can* win that battle, just as you were able to win the battle over your tongue. You may wish to use the exercises in Appendix A and Appendix B to help you).

So now you had the thought, but you curtailed it. It lost a bit of its strength. You can choose to go on to something else. The next time envy or jealousy arise, you do exactly the same. And again and again and again. As you do this, the strength of the neural pathways that have to do with this particular habit will diminish. Eventually the habit will cease. All you have to do is remain conscious enough to practice this. And of course you *have* to want it. It's that easy. And you open the path to joy.

Imagine children jumping for joy. It's an image we often associate with children (or animals), but not so often with ourselves. When is the last time you jumped like that? Or even if you are elderly or confined to a wheelchair, when is the last time you *felt* like jumping like that?

So what has happened to us? I certainly remember jumping for joy as a child and now, as a boomer, my jumps tend to be more in my head, but I feel great joy with simple things - such as having a wonderful coffee in the morning in a spot with a fabulous view (and that can be the view out of the French doors in my living room), but it can also be the view I imagine myself seeing in the breathtaking images I've frequently posted on social media enjoying a virtual coffee at some of the most amazing places in the world. I can also experience great joy as I unfold a newspaper in front of that (real) coffee and settle down to read it (I've noticed the joy is less intense if the newspaper is virtual, in my smart phone, as opposed to feeling a *real* paper in my hands, and hearing the crackle of the sheets).

Other things that bring me great joy are setting out for a weekend drive with a friend (even if it's a short one) into the unknown, or into the countryside, or up into the mountains, or along the Mediterranean, here where I live. I also experience joy as I open a new book, drive to the airport to pick up one of my sons (that's one of the greatest joys!), or as I contemplate an upcoming holiday. Joy comes as well as I savor the aroma of freshly-baked bread (even if I don't always partake), the perfume of jasmine, the tang of the sea, or the unmistakable childhood smells of freshly-mown grass, and the distinctive *eau-de-cologne* my grandmother used.

As you see, my joys are simple. I could list others that cost money or are complicated and involved to achieve, but the fact is, because many of my joys are so simple to attain, I can easily have a number of them every day. And having joy every day, mentally jumping for joy every single day should be on your to-do list in the same taken-for-granted way as you brush your teeth and have a shower. Abraham states: *The standard of success in life isn't the things. It isn't the money or the stuff, it is absolutely the amount of joy you feel* and I totally agree. And so you have to continually ask yourself the question: Am I feeling joy today?

Clearly our inner dialogue and the way we self-soothe is a large part of *what changes* when we begin to love ourselves, leading to not only a healthier life from the physical, psychological, emotional and spiritual point of view, but also leading to a life that is simply so much more wonderful and filled with endless possibilities of joy and well-being.

Your Relationship to Yourself

Having a relationship with yourself is another fundamental change that occurs as you begin to love yourself. It makes sense, doesn't it? After all, if you hold someone in high esteem, it stands to reason that you have a relationship with that person, or, at the very least, you would like to have one. And once you begin to love the self and hold the self in high esteem, obviously you also seek to have a relationship with yourself. You recognize that such a relationship is essential and furthermore, and most importantly, you *want* this relationship. *How could you not want it?*

In the process of recognizing this and getting there, here are some of the steps you may go through, as you question heretofore held ideas of yours:

- How do you feel about your body?
    - Do you really love it? Maybe not. But even if you don't, is it not true that you always take very good (or reasonably good) care of it?
    - And don't you always dress it as well and as beautifully as possible?
    - And you furthermore take care of your hair, your skin, and your nails to look as good as possible, right?
    - How about being that *loving* way with YOU?

In oneself lies the whole world and if you know how to look and learn, the door is there and the key is in your hand. Nobody on earth can give you either the key or the door to open, except yourself.
Jiddu Krishnamurti

- How do you feel about a small child? Especially *your* small child, or perhaps a grandchild or niece or nephew or favorite neighbourhood child?
    - Isn't it true that you love it? And that you always behave lovingly towards it, at least on those occasions when you are with it?
    - Do you shout at it, criticize it, belittle it and demean it? I imagine not.

    o   How about being that *loving* way with YOU?

- How do you behave with aches and pains when they occur in your body? A headache, a cut, a bruise, an infection, a fever?
  - o   Isn't it true that you always take care of them as quickly as possible?
  - o   How about being that *loving* way with YOU and whatever ails you in your feelings and emotions and thoughts?

- Why do you do all of the above things for those others or your body?
  - o   Partially because you want to be seen as looking as good as possible, but also because you want to ease physical discomfort.
  - o   One of the biggest reasons that you tend to do this very quickly, is because you are very conscious and aware of your body, your looks and all your aches and pains.
  - o   How about being that *loving* way with YOU?

In other words, how about becoming conscious and aware of all that goes on inside of you, because that is the beginning of learning to love the self.

- How do you feel when others trespass your boundaries? And what do you consciously do about it?
- How do you feel when you are stressed? And what do you consciously do about it?
- How do you feel when you are angry, impatient, jealous and afraid? And what do you consciously do about it?

Furthermore, what has changed in your relationship to yourself is that you have undertaken at least some of the following ten steps that set you on your path to loving the self. You know it's not necessary to overwhelm yourself by attempting to undertake all ten steps at once. So you began by just tackling those that seemed most amenable to your current state of being and then in the fullness of time continued on to others when you felt you could:

Step #1

Becoming conscious and aware. Simply by doing that alone you began to show yourself on a subliminal level that you are serious about loving the self. You *had to* pay attention to the state of your feelings. Your intention needed to lead you to becoming conscious and aware at *all times*, knowing that you would get to that place bit by bit.

> Every single one of us can do things that no one else can do; can love things that no one else can love. We are like violins. We can be used for doorstops, or we can make music.
> Barbara Sher

Step # 2

Taking the decision to do something about how you are feeling at all times. This meant that you began to love yourself by learning how to soothe yourself in healthy ways. (There is an entire chapter on soothing the self in my book *Rewiring the Soul*, but if you prefer not to get it right now, you can read about *some* of those soothing mechanisms in the following eight steps of this section).

Step # 3

Using the beauty and gratitude exercise found in Appendix A. It's so brief and simple you can repeat it many times every day.

Step # 4

Using the mindfulness walk found in Appendix B.

Step # 5

Learning how to forgive. By forgiving (and remember, it's *not* condoning), you loosened and eventually severed your energetic connections to the painful or bitter past and so you not only began to live in the present, but you also confirmed and demonstrated to yourself (again) that you love yourself and care enough about yourself to do this.

Step # 6

Letting of the past. Living in the past means that only a portion of you is in the here and now. Your psychic energy is invested in past events and not your present life!

Step # 7

Establishing healthy boundaries. This is one of the most effective ways of having shown yourself you love yourself because *you truly take care of yourself* when you established those healthy boundaries. This empowered you. This gave you energy. This signified that others no longer have power over you, nor will they be able to drain you of your energy.

Step # 8

Learning how to communicate effectively *without* reactivity and blindness, and from a conscious position of self-love and self-responsibility. (Also see my book *The Tao of Spiritual Partnership*).

Step # 9

Spending at least as much time on your inner state of well-being as on the outer one. Who is the *real you*? Is it the 25-year-old or the 40-year-old or the 68-year-old who wears designer clothing, casual, or grunge, who rides a bike to work or drives a Porsche, or is it the *self* that you are attempting to connect to and discover in this process of loving the Self that we are describing here? And if you agree that the *real you* is the latter, then does it not make sense that you dedicate *at least* as much time to it, as to your body, nails, hair, clothes and car buying decisions?

Step #10

Taking responsibility for your own happiness and inner well-being, seeking to reestablish inner balance whenever necessary.

Having taken some or all of these ten steps ensured that your passage to loving the self became a reality because each of the steps is inextricably intertwined with all the others. Each is part of the puzzle to loving the Self, and putting one into motion, began the process of bringing all the others into motion as well. It's part of the *magical circle* referred to in Chapter 7.

Your Relationship to Your Children

The most important thing that changes is that you become an adult! Your age is not an issue. Take a moment to consider how it might have been if you had been parented by two people who truly were mature adults. As you can imagine, I'm not talking about their chronological age when you were born and growing up, but about the sad and yet undeniable fact that most of us are not parented by adults. And most of us are not adults *either* when we become parents. This is due to a lack of psycho-emotional maturity, a lack of living a life of conscious awareness, a lack of having made the conscious decision to take on full responsibility for ourselves in all ways, including what we feel and think, what we say and do, and how we react to any and everything and also due to our socialization, no matter in which corner of the global community we were raised. That's a tall order, as we have already seen in great detail in previous chapters, and yet, that is precisely what changes for your children, when you have begun to love yourself and to put into practice all the things we have been discussing here.

What then happens is that you - the parent (assuming you are one) - begin to have the capacity to be an *adult* parent for your children, as opposed to being another child in the household with all its needs and reactivity and ego. *Do you understand what this means not only for yourself, but most specially, for your children?* It totally changes the panorama. Here are a few potential scenarios:

- One of your children is whining - he/she wants an ice cream while you are at the supermarket. You're frazzled. You try ignoring your child. It doesn't work. The whining continues at a higher volume. People are beginning to look over. You snap and either yell at the child, or he/she gets one on the bottom and a threat that if he/she doesn't stop the whining, there will be no TV at home.

Nothing has a stronger influence psychologically on their environment and especially on their children than the unlived life of the parent.
Carl Gustav Jung

Now, however, imagine you've changed, and have become an adult parent. Same scenario but only up to the part where you are frazzled (yes, even self-loving adult parents can be frazzled). Now, however, you don't ignore your child. You bend down, you speak lovingly but firmly. You set the limits (children feel secure and safe when parents set limits that keep expanding in an age-appropriate manner as time goes on), explaining that whining will not bring about ice cream, but good behavior will, and that there *will* be ice cream for dessert at home. You give your child a little hug or pat on the head, and show the child that he/she *exists* for you; you show that you acknowledge your child, even when you are in a rush and frazzled, because such acknowledgment between the two of you will help your child - one day in the future - become that adult parent him or herself. This is such a gift you are giving! (If you are doing this for the first time and your prior behavior resembled the first alternative described above, it may not work immediately. You will need to "walk your talk" for a while before you achieve the desired results and before your children know you mean business. You may also need to read extensively about healthy boundaries).

- You had a distinctly traumatic and difficult childhood. You have a daughter - now 11 - who has always been very needy on an emotional basis. You feel overwhelmed. You ensure the child has everything she needs on a material level, but you tend to push her away emotionally.

    Now, however, imagine you've changed, and have become an adult parent. Same scenario, but due to the history you already had with your daughter of pushing her away, you begin by talking to her - really talking to her, about yourself. Not from the point of view about how difficult life was for you (which you might have done in your earlier, less adult phase), but from the point of view that you have only now realized how needy that made you yourself and so now you have realized that you have to work harder at being a good parent for her and if she is at an appropriate age for such a request, ask her to be patient with you as you learn how to do this. Such a conversation can create miracles. And furthermore, such a conversation sets the groundwork for your daughter to one day in the future - become that adult parent herself. Part of this is due to your willingness to be transparent and vulnerable with your daughter, but simultaneously keeping *both* of you in a *safe* space, as opposed to a space where you show yourself to be a child, and even potentially a victim. Such behavior with our children (which so many of us indulge in, consciously or otherwise), does *not* give our children the loving security they need.

- You have two sons, just approaching puberty. There is much rivalry - and always has been - and you find it very stressful. One of the two is much more forceful than the other and it has become very difficult to stand up to him when you believe he is behaving unfairly to his brother. So basically your attitude is to ignore them, or to shout at them when they go too far, or to punish them, but in an inconsistent fashion.

    Now, however, imagine you've changed, and have become an adult parent. Same scenario, but due to their age, and your past history with them, you now take them aside at a time when they are not battling to be top dog. You begin a dialogue in which you may tell them you believe you've been handling it poorly thus far (one often opens wonderful and magical doors as a parent when one admits one's own shortcomings), and that you believe there has to be a win-win way of dealing with their continual rivalry. You ask them to come and talk to you instead of fighting with each other when things get out of hand, not because you will be judge and juror and arbitrarily decide what should be done, but because you hope to share some negotiating skills with them. You also refer to boundaries and rules everyone will have to abide by, and that if they do not, there will be consequences, and you clearly spell out what those consequences will be (and then, if necessary, if the boundaries continue to be trespassed, you *stick* to those consequences. You tell them that you are having such a conversation with them because you love them and wish to show them how - not only for now as rival brothers, but also for their entire life - they can handle situations that create strife. You let them understand that you know things are not going to change immediately, nor will they change 100%, but that if everyone will do their bit, you are there to help, not to command and punish. You also ask them to help you. What could *you* do differently, in order to help them avoid their difficult situations with each other. Such dialogue coming from a parent to children may also create miracles. And furthermore, such a conversation sets the groundwork for your sons to one day in the future become that adult parent themselves.

- One of your children is having a difficult time at school. There is occasional bullying. Yet you seem to have the perfect family and perfect children. It just doesn't make sense. Eventually you take your story to a therapist and are asked to bring your spouse. Over the course of the conversation, due to what you are recounting as a couple and the gentle questions you are asked, the therapist suggests your husband has poor boundaries. It is therefore recommended that this needs to be looked at in the context of the family dynamic. In order to help all members of the family to move forward more quickly, as opposed to only attempting to work on it at home, perhaps a few family sessions might be in order. This would help not only to move your husband forward (and perhaps yourself because if one spouse has poor boundaries, it is very possible that the other tends to trespass them - although this is not a firm and fast rule), but potentially to help your daughter deal with the bullying at school. Both your husband's poor boundaries and the fact that your daughter is being bullied, point to some lack of self-love in both individuals and perhaps even in all members of the family. You make no immediate decisions, but you never call the therapist to make another appointment, nor do you actively encourage all concerned to work on these issues at home. The whole thing makes you feel rather uncomfortable, and you tell yourself that your husband's poor boundaries aren't really so bad, and that your daughter's bullying at school has more to do with awful kids who also go there and poor teachers, than with any lack of self-love on your daughter's part. And certainly, it simply makes no sense to you that she might have started on this path of lacking self-love because it is not being mirrored to her in the family. You simply prefer not to think about it all.

Now, however, imagine you've changed, and have become an adult parent. Same scenario up to the part where family sessions are suggested by the therapist. You immediately recognize that this is a very important step for the health of the family. While there is some resistance in you about following the suggestion, you nevertheless determine that it may bring benefits for all concerned. You explain your reasoning to your husband and daughter and make an appointment. You do this despite the fact that the whole things continues to make you feel uncomfortable, simply because you know it will be one of the ways to create greater well-being for all members of the family. And by so doing, you set examples for your children and your partner, and this paves the road for all of you to live your lives in a much more conscious and self-loving way than you did up to this point.

We could therefore say that what the power of your heart and the process of loving yourself has changed in the way you deal with and relate to your children, is that you have become self-aware and self-responsible. That signifies that when they push your buttons, for example, the awareness you have achieved *because* you have practiced loving yourself means that you will *not* become reactive. Rather, you will remain in the loving, kind and compassionate position of the *adult* who has chosen to learn to love himself in order that he will be capable of loving his children in the way they deserve (which will include healthy boundaries and specific limitations).

Your Relationship to Your Partner

Perhaps one of the other changes with the greatest and most direct impact that takes place when you begin to love yourself is how you relate to others - in particular how you relate to your partner. Many things fall into place that were either non-existent before, or simply so marginalized with regards to the amount of attention you paid to them, that they made little difference to you. As we've already seen, loving the self implies a broad array of behaviors such as being conscious and aware of yourself, taking on responsibility for yourself in all ways, understanding that you always have a choice, and so forth. Therefore these elements signify that how you now relate to your partner has undergone a metamorphosis. Not all at once, of course, but the more you remain on this road, the more it will happen, and the more you will come to appreciate that this new way of relating spells so much inner freedom, which in turn allows you to love in an entirely different way.

People tend to fall in love with someone who - on the surface - is their idea of, if not the ideal partner, at least close to what they are looking for in a partner - but who underneath the surface - fulfills some of their more important needs. This is a dangerous path to be on in a relationship, and more so, if you are not aware of it, as generally tends to be the case. It's dangerous, simply stated, and as we've seen, because as long as you depend on another to fulfill your needs, or some of your needs, you are not free. I'm not talking about being free of others in the sense of not wanting to be with others but in the sense of not needing them for your inner well-being, because you are able to create that for yourself. The benefit of such a life is that you love from a position of independence rather than from one of dependence.

> Appreciation and self-love are the most important tools that you
> could ever nurture. Appreciation of others and the appreciation of
> yourself is the closest vibrational match to your Source Energy
> of anything that we've ever witnessed.
> Abraham

Think for a moment of the one you love (or loved at some other time of your life). What happened inside of you if that person was annoyed or moody? Did something in you shrivel, cringe, worry? Or did something in you desperately make you try to 'fix' whatever it was that was going on with your partner? Or did something in you immediately assume that the reason your partner was in a bad mood was because of something *you* had done? Clearly, in this example (and there are many other versions), your happiness and inner well-being are so wrapped up in your partner's state of being, that you are in a sense enslaved - even though your partner may have never asked you to be this way.

Another example is when your sense of confidence and security is connected to the degree of control you have over your partner. In a way, this example has the same common denominator as the earlier one, simply because at the root of it all, your happiness and inner well-being depend on how secure your partner makes you feel as long as you believe he/she is behaving in a way that you need for you to be able to feel that security and confidence. This means, of course, that you will always be checking up on him/her, calling frequently, trying to control who is in his/her life, what activities he/she participates in, etc. Once again, as in the earlier example, your happiness and inner well-being are so fully wrapped up in your partner's state of being, that you are in a sense enslaved - even though your partner may have never asked you to be this way.

> The courage to be is the courage to accept oneself,
> in spite of being unacceptable.
> Paul Tillich

Yet another situation that occurs with frequency (and you may - initially - laugh when you read this), is how immensely good we feel and lovable we believe ourselves to be when we are with the beloved. You may ask me in astonishment what could possibly be wrong with such a scenario? It's this: if you feel this way *whether you have a partner or not*, then there is nothing wrong with it. Quite the contrary, in that case, I would shake your hand to congratulate you on a life well lived.

However, when those good or 'being lovable' feelings only emerge when you are with your partner and feel safe and secure because you firmly believe that he/she does indeed love you, but you tend to fall apart when something is amiss in the relationship (even if it's only a lifted eyebrow, or a dark mien, as in the first example here), then we have all the indicators that you are in this relationship because something in your partner fulfills needs for you that you are meant to have learned how to fulfill yourself. And so the most likely scenario that will ultimately occur for you, is that you will find yourself being abandoned in some fashion by the partner, suffer intense emotional pain, feel, perhaps, strong sensations of anger and a desire for revenge, feel victimized, abused, etc., only to possibly repeat this pattern again with another partner or two - until you wake up and realize that it is *you* who are meant to make you feel this way and not your partner. Just as in the earlier examples, your happiness and inner well-being are so wrapped up in your partner's state of being, that you are in a sense enslaved - even though your partner may have never asked you to be this way.

And of course the manner in which you find your way out of this miasma is precisely as indicated earlier. You begin by becoming conscious of your need for another's behavior dictating your well-being. This is not about a partner who no longer fulfills your expectations, or a partner who is not doing (or refusing to do) what you would wish them to do, but about you, because it is *you* who is not taking care of - in a loving way - your own needs. To truly commence walking this path it is necessary to become aware, recognize that you always have a choice, become self-responsible and self-loving. A brief summation of these four fundamental concepts for a life of inner freedom, filled with inner well-being, peace, harmony, and joy follows:

Being Aware: Without awareness there is no self-reflection. Without self-reflection you are unable to comprehend what happens to you other than in knee-jerk fashion. Hence it is paramount that you begin to become aware of all you feel, think, say and do, as well as all your reactions to events and others in order that you may be able to *exercise choice* at all times. If someone insults you and you are not aware, you will react blindly and insult back. If you are aware, you may choose to ignore the person, or reply in another fashion that does not put your inner well-being at stake. By being aware you *know* yourself in ways someone who is not aware does not. Therefore when you are attracted to someone you will begin to pay very close attention to many factors, both within you and within the other. This alone will put you on a totally different path than someone who does not pay attention and simply *falls in love.*

Recognizing That You Always Have a Choice: The only people that don't believe they always have a choice are those who have not yet taken the other steps to growth and self-loving discussed here. Recognizing that you always have a choice - at least in how you choose to react to any given circumstance, inner or outer - is a by-product of becoming conscious, self-responsible, and loving the self. The fact that you take this on board means that you will always be free, because if you always have a choice, you can never be imprisoned or enslaved - at least not in your mind. Think of Mandela in his prison, Frankl in his concentration camp, or Christopher Reeve in his wheel chair.

Being Self-Responsible: Without taking on responsibility for the self in all ways: being responsible for what you think, feel, say, and do, and how you react to all that occurs in your life, you will never truly be free because you will continually place the responsibility (blame) for what occurs on someone or something, and likewise, you will place the responsibility for how you think and feel on others or on specific circumstances. Further, you will never truly find inner peace for all the same reasons. Therefore, when you take the conscious decision to become truly responsible for the self, you begin to live a life where it is indeed possible to love without needing.

Loving the Self: Without recognizing the fundamental and primordial need to love the self, and doing so consciously, step by step, by learning how to do so by taking on responsibility for the self and all that the self feels and thinks, as mentioned above, you will not find true joy, inner peace, and freedom, because you will *not be taking true and loving care of yourself.* When you feel out of sorts, angry, impatient, or anything other than being in a space of inner well-being, loving the self means that you will take care of that feeling and do something about it in order to shift your inner energy in order that you may at the very least find yourself in a space of inner balance and tranquility. In similar fashion, if you find that you are reacting to something - *anything* - in a way that is creating turmoil of any kind, loving the self again means that you will take loving care of the self in order to once again come - at the very least - to a place of inner balance. As we have seen over and over again in this book, loving the self is one of the behaviors that most people are lacking in and is, perhaps, the most important one of all to learn. By loving the self, the other three - being aware, recognizing choice, and being self-responsible - fall into place, because it is impossible to love the self without them.

As you continue to love yourself, simultaneously making it a more and more automatic aspect of your life, your relationship to your partner changes in numerous minute daily details, but the majority of those details will fall under the general umbrella of the above-described themes. Your reactivity will have vanished, or, even if it has not yet been totally eradicated from your behavior, you will be conscious enough to immediately take it in hand when it makes itself known. Your moods - that could affect the tenor of your interaction with your partner - are a thing of the past. You no longer need to be right because your ego has taken a long hike, you no longer need to criticize or judge because you have learned how to communicate, and your fears of vulnerability - although perhaps still very much present - are being dealt with by the transparency of your new mode of communication and, perhaps more importantly, are being dealt with by your own inner burgeoning sense of security that is no longer dependent on another, but rests in you. It always comes back to *you*, and what is different now is that you have recognized it and taken it on board. This is being conscious, this is caring for and loving the self and this brings you to the gates of inner freedom, peace, and harmony.

Your Relationship to Your Life

Loving the self has major implications regarding the manner in which you relate to your life. Think for a moment of how you used to deal with your demons. There's hardly anyone who hasn't got some. Perhaps they're due to those traumatic childhood memories. Or maybe they weren't traumatic, just not very nice, such as your mother who never stopped judging and criticizing you. Or perhaps it was your father who expected so much of you that you wound up never being good enough. How about the schoolyard bully that left your self-confidence and self-esteem shaken? Did your best friend from first grade betray you and forsake your company for that other kid whose toys were shinier, or cookies better, or whose mom allowed them to stay up until midnight on sleepovers?

Whatever your demons were, they would tend to plague you, and so obviously, you had to find ways to deal with them. That might have been by having a drink (or several) too many on too many occasions in order to feel less unloved, or insecure. It might be that you never drank, but that you worked too much, losing your feelings of inadequacy in that work and the success it brought you. Or perhaps you took too many walks to the refrigerator, or helped yourself with a little white pill that took off the edge, or perhaps you spent too many hours at the gym every week, or perhaps those excess hours were spent at mass, or in an ashram, and so you forgot about actually *living* your life, or you needed to run marathons just a little too often. This meant that red flags were waving, indicating that you were using these - or other - activities in order to tamp down the anxiety, perhaps even panic inside of you. You used them to deal with low-grade depressions, with fear, and any number of other emotions that assailed you - and probably had assailed you since you were small - that you simply didn't know what to do with.

The red flags signaled another kind of message as well: they told you that you had not yet connected with yourself. They told you that self-love was missing. They told you that they (the red flags) were there *in order that you might begin to change something in your life so that those anxiety-ridding activities no longer be necessary* (at least not for *that* reason), *but also in order that you realized that as long as you depended on those activities, you were never dealing with the underlying issues.* And of course the word 'issues' simply meant that you needed to begin by picking up your courage, leaving your comfort zone, and beginning to become aware, more loving, and more self-responsible. The most important reason why you needed to start to clean up your act was this: as long as you did not rid yourself of the mechanisms you had used to that point in your life that helped you deal with your fears, anxieties, or feelings of inadequacy - *you were never going to be able to truly be yourself.* You were never going to be able to truly accomplish most of what you *could* accomplish, because *most of your energy would have been used to take care of those negative feelings - those demons.* They splintered you, they fragmented you, and they kept you tied to the past. And that, of course, was reason enough to start with this process, so that the phoenix would be able to arise from the ashes of those demons. That is how loving yourself is able to change your relationship to your life.

Another vital aspect that changes is that you began to look at your own *inner* growth as a goal. Excellent seminars are available globally that teach the planning and eventual achieving of goals. We all understand how important it is to *plan* and map out our goals. But those goals tend to refer to our professional, economic, or academic success, perhaps our success in sports, or in turning a rather large and flabby body into a sleeker, slimmer and more toned one.

But prior to this process of beginning to love the self looking at your own *inner* growth as a goal was not something that was frequently found on the agenda. Once you begin to do it, it implies also setting up a plan and mapping out your goals in this other, much less tangible and certainly less outwardly visible sense.

People are crying up the rich and variegated plumage of the peacock, and he is himself blushing at the sight of his ugly feet.
Sa'Di

And so some of the things - some of the steps - that this process would entail might have looked like what follows. In no specific order, here is a list - by no means all-encompassing - that you may have considered as starting points:

- If you still watch television, you would spend *at least* as much time as you spend watching it, either reading books that further your inner growth (all my books offer an extensive Bibliography and many of those books listed there are superb exemplars you can start with), or watching videos (or listening to audio clips) of seminars and talks you can both purchase or freely acquire on the internet, by inspirational and motivating speakers with whom you resonate. Obviously this means that if you were spending two hours watching television every day and then another two hours reading or listening to seminars, you might have found yourself in a time bind. Hopefully this would have encouraged you to happily shorten your television viewing time by a considerable amount. (For some sample ideas see Appendix D).

- You would have begun to think deeply about the people with whom you spend your free time. Do they further your growth? Perhaps you further theirs and that is excellent, but you will also need to develop relationships with some people who further yours. Beware of spending *empty* hours talking about *empty* subjects. *You are worth so much more.*

- You would have developed some kind of inner work along the lines of a meditation practice or a mindfulness practice. (also see Appendix B) Remember that in order to connect to yourself, you need to *know* that self, and this - being still in the present moment - is one of the best ways of going in that direction.

- You might have begun to pay attention to your dreams, to write them down, to honor them, and to learn how to interpret them. Jung wrote: *The dream is a little hidden door in the innermost and most secret recesses of the psyche.*

- You would have begun to spend time in nature, preferably every day, noticing that it affects your energy and your spirit, directly impacting on your energetic frequency. You would have begun using nature to commune with yourself.

- You would have spent some time giving your brain and body extra oxygen, preferably every day. This means some kind of exercise, even if it's only walking (which, by the way, is an excellent exercise).

- You would have spent time learning how to truly communicate with those you love. This is not only an investment in your relationships with those people, but also an investment in yourself in the sense that it allows you to further connect to yourself.

- You might have begun to keep a journal - knowing that it would be a remarkable record for you to compare where you are now - at whatever point in the future - as opposed to where you were when you began the journal. You might have been amazed at how far you have come. Looking back at such a trajectory in your own life is frequently very motivating when you are faced with new challenges - on any level.

- You probably began to *intend* to forgive wherever needed in all those not yet forgiven parts of your life. You would have recognized that you needed to *intend* to not only forgive those who have transgressed against you, but also to forgive yourself, for surely you have also transgressed against others.

- You would make a point of finding joy every day.

- You would do something at least once a day (preferably much more than that) that shows you that you love yourself. You would care for yourself and be gentle, loving, and forgiving with yourself.

- You would practice being aware as much as you can during your day, every day.

- You would practice making conscious choices. You would know that you *always have a choice.*

- You would practice being aware of yourself when you felt the need to be right, or when you were being judgmental or critical, and once you recognized these *habits* in yourself, you would practice getting rid of them. *Do you really want your ego being your spokesperson* or do you prefer to speak for yourself?

- You would practice learning to be responsible for yourself by taking responsibility for your thoughts, feelings, words, actions and reactions.

- You would practice (yes - *practice*) being loving, kind, and compassionate, even when you didn't feel like it.

- You would tell yourself at least once a day that we are all one - where I end, you begin, and vice versa. You would have clearly understood that the I - you dyad is no longer viable for you.

- You would use every situation that presents itself to you as an opportunity to learn and grow.

The simple change in direction when you begin to love the Self puts so much into motion. The way you then relate to yourself and your life, and the way you then self-reflect and seek congruency in your connection to yourself and your life is one of the most profound manifestations of this miraculous transformation.

Love, Kindness & Compassion: We Are All One

Can you even begin to imagine that once you start walking down the road of loving the self, that you would ever consider another being less worthy of love than yourself? To be absolutely fair, as a matter of fact most people do continue to think of others - or some others - as being less worthy of love, and most particularly, most continue to see themselves as separate from others, and most certainly, *not* as one with others. But - and this is the crux of the matter, it is in this arena where potentially the highest and most *enlightened* order of transformation and change is eventually produced.

You see, as you continue working on loving yourself, on caring for yourself in the way we have spent so much time discussing in this book, you begin to recognize that loving the self may *begin* with you, but it leads to love of *all others*. You begin to recognize a need for becoming much more loving, kind and compassionate with others - all others - and you yearn to understand how to bring this about in your own being. With that yearning, you are well on the road to accepting that we are all one, and having accepted it as a premise, you take it into your heart and soul. This transformation is the most profound of all.

> If you don't love yourself, you will not be able to love others. If you have no compassion for yourself then you are not able to develop compassion for others.
> Dalai Lama

Have you ever noticed that when you are not in the best of moods, or when you are upset or resentful or angry about something, you seem to find *more* people who actually create *even more* of those feelings in you? Almost as though a tuning fork were set to ensure that those people with negative feelings that exactly match yours cross your path that day at exactly the same time as you are there! As a matter of fact, when I was younger this happened at a certain point with such frequency that I deliberately started paying attention to it. It had grabbed, you might say, my attention, because it was happening too often to be put down to mere coincidence. *Was*, I asked myself, *the universe playing with me*?

As I became aware of all of this, I also began noticing that when I was in a good place inside myself, I seemed to bring more people with that kind of *mood*, or inner vibration into my sphere during that day. It also seemed to be a lot more difficult to make me lose my equanimity, to become upset about anything, or to engage in hostility or negativity.

So, I thought, this must mean that depending on how I feel, and perhaps on what I emanate, just by virtue of what can be seen or felt by those who are in my vicinity, I attract an entirely different kind of experience or person into my life. Therefore it appeared not to be a bad idea to decide that I live in a *friendly universe*, a term I have borrowed from Einstein *and* Wayne Dyer. A universe in which it is *just as easy* to run into friendly people as it is to run into angry people, *just as easy* to run into helpful people as it is to run into impatient and unkind people, *just as easy* to run into positive and joyful people, as it is to run into negative and unhappy people.

And although the connection is wide, as I revisit this topic in order to write this section, it immediately made me think of a book titled *Brain Rules* by neuroscientist John Medina, who after writing many chapters jam-packed with scientific detail about the brain and how to best understand how it works and how to deal with it, expresses wonder and amazement near the end of the book describing his young son one day as he accompanies him to his nursery school. They were walking a short distance that would have taken Medina father a few minutes to cover, but because he was escorting the small child, it took much longer. But mainly it took so long - and this was the source of the father's wonder - because his son stopped at every blade of grass, as if to observe its growth, or to examine how it had emerged from a minute crack in the cement of the sidewalk, or to become totally absorbed in the inspection of an ant as it shouldered its load of one bread crumb on its way to the underground colony, following a long line of its brethren.

Medina realized his child was much more present than he himself tended to be, and although he does not use the term *mindfulness* in his book, I do, because I believe that is *precisely* what a child does, and what we adults tend not to do, and hence we find it so much harder to decide that we are living in a friendly universe.

> I have found that the greatest degree of inner tranquility comes from the development of love and compassion. The more we care for the happiness of others, the greater is our own sense of well-being. Cultivating a close, warmhearted feeling for others automatically puts the mind at ease. It is the ultimate source of success in life.
> Dalai Lama

As we arise in the morning, we already make decisions about the day in question:

- oh no, it's raining
- oh no, it's not raining
- oh no, it's so cold
- oh no, it's so hot

And of course, the real problem does not lie with the condition of the weather, but *our inner resistance to what is.* Krishnamurti said that the secret to his happiness was *not minding what happens*, and I have repeated this frequently in workshops, talks and other writing, because I believe beyond a shadow of a doubt that it contains endless wisdom. It does *not* mean becoming apathetic, but it *does* mean accepting what is, finding inner balance and peace with regards to that, and *only then* deciding what needs - or can - be done about it, rather than embarking on reactions and actions based on a feeling of resistance to what is.

So if we set out on our day with an attitude of acceptance, and then go to the wonder and joy of the child, perhaps we will hear the brilliant birdsong as we open the window, or see the ray of sunshine amidst the grey, as it attempts to slice a cloud in half. And as we do so, we notice our inner energetic vibration being in a good place, and we are aware of the fact, not only due to research in a multitude of disciplines, but also because of how we feel on this more visceral, physical level, that our inner mindset is also affecting the state of our cells, our very biology.

And so we progress throughout our day, looking for the many reasons that the universe is indeed a friendly place, filled with events, and sights, and people and moments that can quicken our heart with joy and well-being - *if only we decide*.

You get to decide whether you live in a hostile or a friendly universe. You can decide what each of the things that happens every day mean. You get to decide whether your life is good or bad *no matter how it may look on the outside*. Remember what I've said so often about Viktor Frankl or Nelson Mandela or the innumerable others who have gone through great suffering, and yet have made a choice about how their life is going, and especially *how they are going to look at it, think about it, and hence, feel about it, and react to it*.

It's also true that the more you look for reasons to believe that things are going against you, and that people don't like you or accept you, the less you will be disappointed in your expectations.

And don't forget that *your thoughts* - as molecular and cellular biology show us - *really do become things*, so the manner in which you view your world *and think about it* is of great importance.

As I've pointed out so frequently: you choose.

You can choose to wake up in the morning and be grateful for the new day and new opportunities. You can choose to remember to be grateful every day about something and someone in your life, and to make a habit of this - without fail - in order to help keep your mind on that instead of what you didn't like. You can choose to find something of value to you and your life in whatever it is that you didn't like, even if it is learning how to choose not to react negatively in the face of adversity.

You choose.

So by loving yourself and deciding to live in a friendly universe you move closer to a position of lovingness, kindness and compassion for all by choosing the way that is of use to you, instead of the way that simply increments the negative. And in this friendly universe you find all those beings with whom you sense a deep connection because you've recognized that we are indeed all one. And therefore you understand that what you do and think and feel may have an effect on all others, just as what they do, think, and feel may have an effect on you. And so you begin to live your life according to a new paradigm that is ruled by love. It begins with self-love and ends with love, kindness, and compassion for all. This is your goal.

You choose.

Chapter 10

Recognizing the Treasure

Wouldn't it be powerful if you fell in love with yourself so
deeply that you would do just about anything if you
knew it would make you happy? This is precisely
how much life loves you and wants you to
nurture yourself. The deeper you love yourself, the
more the universe will affirm your worth. Then you can
enjoy a lifelong love affair that brings you the richest
fulfillment from inside out.
Alan Cohen

The opening statements of this book announced: "It is your
right to live a life of love. It is your right to understand that loving
yourself *first* is not a selfish way of behavior, but one that allows
you to live that life of love", and this is precisely the essence of
what you come to understand and embrace - the treasure that you
recognize - as the process of loving yourself unfolds. The richness -
because you can never again be poor - that now suffuses your inner
being can only grow.

At the beginning you may fear - as has been expressed to me by some of my clients who have been courageous enough to step down this path that so many other people do not - that the treasure you are beginning to glimpse will not last. Ephemeral and evanescent, you may fear it will disappear. Others have told me that they believe that the state of their inner well-being - due to the multiple implications that loving the self bring on board - is illusory, perhaps even delusional, and I assure you - as I have assured them - that nothing could be further from the truth. Once you know how to ride a bicycle, you *always* know. Once you've learned how to shape letters on a page with a pencil, you *always* know. And this is like that.

Once you are able to truly discern the light in you that is eternal and that is simply you and that connects you to all others, then the love and delight you feel for yourself becomes boundless.

Compassion for myself is the most powerful healer of them all.
Theodore Isaac Rubin

Loving the self literally creates a new world for you because although you see the same one you saw before, you now see it with eyes that are able to acknowledge and recognize the infinite beauty that surrounds us all. You see a world filled with possibilities, a world filled with individuals for whom you begin to access your ability to love, to whom you are able to show kindness and compassion because you see them as you see yourself because you understand that we are not separate, and above all, you now have the capacity to see the world - which may be filled with pain and strife - from an inner position of peace and harmony, which signifies that strife simply does not have the power to affect you negatively.

The treasure is composed of a many-faceted jewel. The following sections describe some of these facets, which will only become more and more brilliant as time goes on.

The State of Your Inner Energy

The treasure recognized in knowing that the state of your inner energy is ruled by love spells greater freedom than any you may have known before. The power of your heart - the power of loving yourself - and the power of loving and connecting with the Self, gives you utter autonomy with respect to your inner energy. No one who has not experienced life in this fashion, can truly fathom the extent of liberty this represents for all those who choose to walk down this path.

What prevails in your life? Is it love? Or is it fear? If love is stronger you will know it immediately because in general, your life holds a measure of well-being and peace that - should your life be ruled by fear - you will not be tremendously well acquainted with.

Being ruled by fear necessitates a negative charge to daily life. It means - in simple terms - that you are not confident that you will be fine no matter what occurs. In other words, you are fearful of some things happening, essentially because you believe - you fear - that if they happen, you will suffer. Exactly what those events are that you fear may vary from person to person to such a degree that what John fears most is something that Simon does not fear at all, and yet what Simon fears, is something that John considers a simple challenge that can easily be surmounted. Living a life where at some point - most likely some subconscious point - you chose fear over love *does not mean that you are a coward or a wimp*. This is not about courage. It is about understanding some elementary aspects about the goodness of life and about believing in the self the way one does when one has established a relationship with the

Self. And you only ever do that if you have begun the process of loving the Self.

The fact of the matter is that those things that we fear - as long as we continue to fear whatever they are - can never be fully enumerated, because we have no way of knowing what we may have to face at the next turn of the road. Fear - in this sense - implies wishing to *control* that which we may encounter, and as said, it is never possible to control everything that we *might* encounter, because we simply don't know what we *will* encounter at any given time.

At this point the choice for love and trust in the self may - if we are conscious enough - enter the equation.

> Yours is the energy that makes your world. There are no limitations to the self except those you believe in.
> Jane Roberts

Love has to do with confidence, with caring for the self and with knowing that because you care for the self, you are able to handle things as they arise in your life - even when those things are difficult or painful. More than anything, above all, and in the very first instance, choosing love has to do with *loving the self* and because of this love you possess the firm inner conviction that you can deal with any of the cards that life throws you. That does not mean, by the way, that you will always win or always be successful, or always get what you want. It simply means that no matter what happens, you will be able to deal with it in such a way that your inner well-being remains on an even keel. Look at some of the examples I mention over and over again, who were able to do this: Nelson Mandela who spent 27 years locked up in Robben Island, Viktor Frankl who was imprisoned in Auschwitz and lost almost all members of his family to the gas chambers while he was there, or Aimée Mullins whose legs were both amputated when she was five.

This inner conviction does not come about just in an instance. Let's say you have lived your life driven by fear to this point. You've attempted - often unsuccessfully - to exert a measure of control over those outer circumstances that threaten to throw your well-being off center. You are ruled - to a degree - by the subliminal fear or knowledge that you are not able to control your life, and hence you don't know how you will *be* if something bad happens. You don't know if you will be able to deal with, or even *bear* the circumstances - whatever they may be. This creates – if not outright fear, since fear is such a strong emotion – at least a continual sensation of discomfort under your skin, so to speak. Something about you, concerning your life and the way you live does not feel at ease.

The process of moving from a fear-ruled life in the sense described above to a love-ruled life always begins with the recognition of the need to learn how to love the self. By loving the self, fear gradually begins to dissipate because when your life is ruled by love and when you have chosen love as the primary benchmark for how you live your life, you develop into a person for whom fear – or *dis-ease* - no longer looms large as it does for those who have not yet made such choices.

In this book we have seen the decisive importance of loving the Self over and over, so I now wish to leave you with several thoughts:

- Choosing love over fear signifies that you view your life from the vantage point of goodness, love, strength and hope, as well as peace, love and harmony, as opposed to fear, competition, one-up-man-ship, and the need to prove that something about you, your life or what you do is more right than that of another individual.

- Choosing love over fear means every situation *always* brings you to a win-win end result (although the world may not view it as such).
- Choosing love over fear as an equivalent to a *modus operandi* for your life; a way to live your life that will literally change *everything* for you.
- Choosing love over fear will also change the effect you have on all those whose lives you touch and so *you* will actively - and most literally - contribute to *change our world*.

Choose love. Choose it for you, your loved ones, your neighbourhood, your community, your nation and your world. We are all in this together and we can all contribute to making this change. All it takes is *all of us choosing love over fear.* Remember that we are all one and that what affects one of us, affects us all.

Endless Choice: It's In *Your* Hands

Recognizing the treasure of being able to access endless choice - on an inner level - is profound indeed. As we have been discovering, this signifies that no part of your inner world need ever be anything other than that which you wish it to be, even though your outer world may lie in tatters. Jean Paul Sartre said *we are our choices*, and therein lies the reason why a life filled with self-love as opposed to one that is not contains the treasure to which this chapter refers, because it is precisely in our choices that our life becomes filled with possibility and joy, or borders on despair and hopelessness. Often the *only* choice we have is how we react on that inner level, and because it determines so much of our well-being, it is there that so much of the die is cast. Without self-love this would not be possible.

One of the greatest aspects of the treasure we come to appreciate is that the ego no longer establishes what we need and don't need in order to live a good life. The ego is no longer in charge of our state of well-being, and certainly, no longer in charge of anything at all. You might say, the ego has been eradicated from the life of one who lives on the precepts of healthy self-love. The shackles that are removed by this part of the process alone, release a very heavy weight indeed.

Consider what role the ego plays in the life of anyone who has not yet reached this point of self-love: it is the *ego* that determines that *you have to be right*, or *that you have to know better*, or *that your opinion is the one with value*, and it is also the *ego* that makes you want to be more, have more, be more powerful, more important, and more successful than others. That signifies that as long as you are in thrall of the ego, you are not free. It's as simple as that. You dance according to the tunes it plays, and *not* according to your own tune. And the treasure - as self-love takes over your life - is that the ego no longer has any power over you. It's almost as though an addiction had been removed from your psyche. And as said, it clearly indicates the degree of your self-determination.

We cross infinity with every step; we meet eternity in every second.
Rabindranath Tagore

Another aspect of having endless choice is that *need* no longer forms part of your life - at least not on the level it did before, and this too, is a treasure worth cherishing. No longer being dictated by need goes hand in hand with the ego, because in a sense, it is the ego that plagues you with those continual needs that kept you restless, dependent, and despondent before.

As we've seen, the reason is simple: by loving yourself, you learned how to fulfill your own needs. By fulfilling them yourself, you no longer ask of others, require of others, or need others to fulfill them for you. And the treasure there is - just as when you leave the ego behind - that you attain inner freedom.

Bliss: Knowing You Can Always Be in a State of Well-Being

The treasure here lies in the fact that you have made yourself responsible for that inner state of well-being. *It simply does not depend on others or outer circumstances.* You may have noticed that all the 'treasures' this section refers to, appear to be revolving around the same thing, and to some degree they are. You may recall that earlier in this book I told you that whichever sector of your life you begin to work on, in order to experience love for yourself, you would eventually affect - by so doing - all other sectors of your life. And so it is now with the treasure, because in some fashion, the true treasure is the YOU that you have found by loving the Self.

What follows, are some of the byways and paths you may have found (or still need to find) in order to fully perceive and appreciate your treasure.

Have you ever wondered why others can be heroes and *you are not*? Have you ever felt plagued by a vague sense of uneasiness that seems to be saying that *you could do more*? Or felt bitter because others are openly and publicly recognized for what they have accomplished, and *you are not*? Perhaps you need to consider getting a new pair of glasses.

Over the years I've been greatly inspired by Joseph Campbell, world-renowned mythologist, who in turn, was inspired by another one of my own figurative mentors: Carl Gustav Jung, the Swiss psycho-analyst who so famously broke from Freud, and wrote such an amazing number of books, each more eye-opening than the one before. Campbell spent much of his life writing about the figure of the *hero*, not only the mythological hero, but also the hero who resides in each of us and is begging for release into his particular and individual adventure.

Man can alter his life by altering his thinking.
William James

Campbell notably wrote: *Opportunities to find deeper powers within ourselves come when life seems most challenging.* And that is what being a hero is all is about. So when we seek recognition, it has to first come from our *own* recognition of the hero within - the hero that *each one of us is* on a daily basis, in our own heroic journey. Consider this:

- What did you do that day in the schoolyard when you were only 10 and saw Suzy getting bullied by the two older girls?
- What did you do that day when your car broke down in the middle of nowhere with no reception for your mobile phone?
- What did you do when you found it appeared that your baby had drowned in the pool, but you refused to accept it and fought for his life?
- What did you do when you lost your job due to downsizing, could not find another in your field, but had to pay the bills?
- What did you do when you realized your profession was not fulfilling you, but because of your obligations to family and home, you were not able to simply strike out for something else? Isn't it true that you stayed on, biding your time, and

gave of yourself for the sake of those who depended on you?

- What did you do during the nine months your father was dying of terminal lung cancer to help him ease the discomfort?

Whatever you have done in your life, and not only in moments of challenge such as the examples enumerated above, but also in your quest to give meaning to your life - whether it be by seeking more intrinsically fulfilling work, or by learning how to play the piano, or by studying the mating patterns of sperm whales, or by teaching newly-arrived immigrants in your country your language to help them adapt more quickly - any and all of these examples, as well as all the others your imagination can come up with, show you where you have become a hero in your life. You just have to recognize it.

The snow goose need not bathe to make itself white.
Neither need you do anything but be yourself.
Lao Tzu

You may not wish to be labeled a hero, but you will begin to appreciate yourself much more, and to approve of yourself much more, and to love yourself much more, if you begin to give heroic value to those things that you have done - whatever they may be - that are in the directions I've painted above.

Your heroic behavior deserves recognition and admiration, but sometimes we are the only ones who really know about what we have done. CNN's heroes of the year, an annual program that gives praise and recognition to a few individuals, nevertheless culls those particular heroes from a list that is much, much longer. The fact that some receive such public acknowledgement and others do not, is not particularly important if you become aware of your own heroic qualities.

- Do you sit in a wheelchair all day, dealing with a life from that vantage point, instead of being able to stand on your feet? This too, is being a hero.

- Do you spend the days of your retirement helping young teens at the neighbourhood high school excel in math? This too, is being a hero.

- Do you volunteer at a local shelter or soup kitchen? This too, is being a hero.

- Do you brush away your tiredness after a long day at work in order to come back home and offer your children a smile while you fix them dinner and help them with their homework? This too, is being a hero.

- Do you live a life of grim financial, or physical hardship? And do you get up each morning and set out on your day determined to live positively, determined to look for yet another way out of your predicament, and determined to not allow it to get your down? This too, is being a hero.

- Have you become aware of parts of your personality that do not serve you well? Are you critical, judgmental, unkind, impatient, or arrogant? Making the effort to overcome such ways of thinking and behaving is also being a hero.

- Do you have a dream ... any dream ... and do you make a conscious effort each and every day to make your dream a reality? This too, is being a hero.

Campbell also wrote: *It is by going down into the abyss that we recover the treasures of life. Where you stumble, there lies your treasure.*

So once again, it is in the overcoming of stumbling blocks, it is in facing the darkness (problems, desperation, pain) that we find our rainbow, our inner light, which for the purposes of this chapter I am calling our inner hero.

Recognize your own hero, give yourself approbation and praise for what you have done this far in your life. The inner hero resides in all of us - have you become aware of your own? And in so doing, you will have recognized the bliss of knowing that you can always be in an inner state of well-being? This is the treasure.

Freedom: The Brilliant Light of Dawn

The treasure is you. The treasure is the love you have developed for yourself. The treasure is knowing that this is now a part of you and always will be. It can never be taken away from you and this gives you boundless inner freedom. You now know - and this is another way of looking at the treasure - that no matter what happens, you will be OK. When I tell people about this, they often have a hard time grasping it, because life brings us so many twists and turns, that we never know what we might be faced with next. As we've seen, that creates fear in many: fear of losing a loved one, fear of losing financial security, fear of aging, fear of ill health, fear of dying, not to mention the innumerable variations of possibilities apart from these few that I've listed. *That fear stems from a lack of self-love.* It stems from a life lived in fear instead of in love. The inner strength that arises simultaneously with self-love is the strength that will - at that moment in your future - allow you to face challenges (even very tough challenges) from a position of inner peace and harmony. Does that mean you will be able to shrug things off and forget about them? No. But it means that the equanimity with which you view those challenges comes from the freedom that you have achieved thanks to your self-love.

This is so much more than financial freedom; so much more than the freedom power may give you; so much more than the freedom a firm, strong, youthful body may give you, because this freedom can be found whether your body is infirm and living in a wheelchair, or whether your finances only permit you to live in a small apartment. The freedom that is based on loving the Self *depends on no one and nothing at all other than you and your inner connection to the Self that you have learned to love.*

The treasure found in knowing that you are free is endless and eternal. The freedom stems from the love you have found for yourself and for the Self, and from the knowledge that this love connects you to all others. This means you are able to internalize that we are truly all one, and that the exquisite beauty of your own Self is as brilliant as the beauty of all.

I wish I could show you, when you are lonely or in darkness,
the astonishing light of your own being.
Hafiz

APPENDIX A

Brief Beauty & Gratitude Exercise

While this exercise is very similar to the mindfulness walk in Appendix B, it differs in that it can be done at any time, in any place, and in less than one minute, and without anyone actually noticing that you are doing it. Whenever you need to find a momentary space of inner peace (and the more often you practice this exercise, the more quickly and strongly the sensation of peace will come to you), simply do this exercise.

Look about you. Find something beautiful, preferably nature, but it can be anything. Perhaps you see a tree, a cloud, or a flowering bush. Perhaps you see sunshine, or drops of rain, or a snowflake. Perhaps you look at a plant in the room in which you find yourself, a painting, a rug, or an object you admire. Focus on this thing of beauty, really letting yourself see it, and then allow yourself to feel gratitude for having it in your life at this moment. As you feel the gratitude, notice a small sensation of peace in your solar plexus.

Each time you do this, a new neural pathway in your pre-frontal cortex begins to form and strengthen. Therefore, each subsequent time you do it, you will notice the sensation of peace a bit more, and it may last a bit longer.

Furthermore, the more you practice this at *any* time during your day, the more it will begin to permeate your life at odd moments, when you are *not* practicing it, but when you might need that moment of peace and inner calm.

APPENDIX B

15-Minute Mindfulness Walk

Choose a time, during daylight hours when you can walk unimpeded, on your own, for 15 minutes. Start by focusing on the beauty around you, whether this is beauty you see, smell, hear, taste or touch. When you do this, also allow yourself to feel gratitude for whatever it is you are perceiving with one or more of your senses. This brings you into the present moment, allowing your mind to be still. Then do it again, by noticing something else, and again, feel the gratitude. Try to continue doing this for the entire 15 minutes. If at one point you realize your thoughts have wandered off to your worries or past pain, or just everyday problems, don't get annoyed with yourself. Simply pull yourself back to noticing beauty again until your 15 minutes are up.

Just as in the beauty and gratitude exercise of Appendix A, new neural pathways are formed and strengthened each time you practice the mindfulness walk. This exercise builds on the beauty exercise, and when both are used in conjunction with one another, this section of your brain that has a great deal to do with inner well-being, and the speed with which you can 'switch' over to it, will grow in strength even more quickly.

APPENDIX C

Time Line Exercise

Sample

YEAR: 2003   AGE: 32

Address	Lived With	School / Job
22 Market Rd Carville, IN	John (husband, age 35), Sally (daughter, age 6) Cuddles (cat)	Just returned to work at a law firm after 6 years absence

Important Events that year (from birthday to birthday)

- My sister Karen spend part of the year with us as she was getting a divorce and had no where to stay. This caused tension between John and me, although Sally loved having her around

- John's father had a serious car accident and was laid up for months. John flew out to see him in Houston every so often and that strained our finances.

- Sally bloomed at school and we were so endlessly proud of her.

- Our neighbors on the left side of the house built an extension and so we had construction noise for months and this caused some friction between them and us.

- The fact that I had gone back to work was a relief for me for several reasons: it helped our financial situation and it allowed me to get out of the house that I had started to hate due to the noise and the restrictive life I led there since Sally's birth.

- On one of John's trips to Houston to see his father, he was offered a job by one of his father's business associates and so when he returned we spent some time weighing the pros and cons of moving, selling the house, me needing to find a new job at another firm, and so on.

- That was also the year that I decided to learn how to play tennis, because I realized I had to do something physical.

- As I write this, I see the change in my relationship with Sally since then - I see her as a miracle in my life now, instead of a restriction.

Note:

- You can see how these bland facts, that you may not have forgotten, will, nevertheless, as you write them down as you remember that they took place that year, show you that as you turned 32, you had a rather difficult year. You probably grew more patient and perhaps tolerant due to the different situations that went on. Perhaps the year before you had planted a garden that you were very proud of and that had offered you a great deal of relaxation despite the hard work, but you were very unhappy to leave it - more than your job - when John told you about the offer in Houston. As you examine this, you realize how connected you were to the earth, and you remember how much Sally loved helping you there.

- This simple exercise - of just looking at *one* of the years of your life in hindsight - is offering you insight into yourself, your evolution, your growth and progress. Because of this, you may be seeing yourself in ways you had not before, because you are coming to know yourself in this relatively small way.

- Furthermore, it allows you some practice in the art of self-reflection

APPENDIX D

Sample Talks

- Wayne Dyer: The Power of Intention
  - http://www.youtube.com/watch?v=PBdf0sCXYJI
- Caroline Myss: Why People Don't Heal (This has 8 short parts)
  - http://www.youtube.com/watch?v=7kGZfZsTYgo
- Bruce Lipton / Wayne Dyer
  - http://www.youtube.com/watch?v=BiXD6ySST8U
- Steve Jobs: How to live before you die
  - http://www.ted.com/talks/steve_jobs_how_to_live_before_you_die.html
- Bruce Lipton: The power of thought and consciousness
  - http://www.youtube.com/watch?v=C1WygtgxLPc
- Ken Robinson says schools kill creativity
  - http://www.ted.com/talks/ken_robinson_says_schools_kill_creativity.html
- Mattieu Ricard on Google Tech Talks: Change your Mind, Change your Brain: The Inner Conditions For Authentic Happiness
  - http://www.youtube.com/watch?v=L_30JzRGDHI
- How To Find And Do Work You Love:
  - http://www.youtube.com/watch?v=jpe-LKn-4gM

APPENDIX E

Self & self

I have hesitated to offer any definition for the difference between *self* and *Self*, but it appears I have no choice, although any words I use incur the risk of being far too narrow. In the sense that I am using it in this book *self* refers to the mundane, finite, and physical self - that part of us that we can see and touch and hear and physically experience. It is the part that learns and studies and laughs and cries and ages. However, the way in which I am using *Self,* it refers to our eternal part, our divine Self, our soul, that which always was and always will be. It is that which is one with all, and simultaneously *derives from* the Source and *is* the Source.

BIBLIOGRAPHY

In my book *Rewiring the Soul* I included about 40 pages of Bibliography prefaced with the following words:

Why does a book as deceptively simple as this one require such an extensive bibliography? It doesn't. Nevertheless, these books are a portion of those that have shaped my life and in so doing have shaped my thoughts and my understanding. And it is in the shaping of these that this book could be written so simply and so directly. Psychology, neuroscience, biology, sociology, history, politics, religion, spirituality, philosophy, mythology, dreams and fairy tales, body work, metaphysics and esoteric thought, motivational books, biographies and autobiographies all form part of this mélange, as well as some journals of certain writers or thinkers and several dozen novels that have also been included because they too, were significant.

I have returned over and over again to some of these books, as one returns to old and loved friends; friends that are beloved because of what has been shared and because of the support that has been given, and what has been learned. Sometimes, however, I return to a book, no longer certain if I remember it, and then I see the highlighting, the underlining and the scribbled notes on *precisely* those passages that still resonate with me now, and that reminded me then, when I first read them, of what I really already knew. *Just as you do.* It's not really important if you look at this list at all. But perhaps you'll enjoy doing so.

The Power of Your Heart: Loving the Self is built on those books as well, because as I say above, these books shaped me and my thinking over the course of my life. But I hope you understand that in order to keep the publishing cost of this book down, those many pages will not be included again.

However, you can access them all here online by going to this link: http://tinyurl.com/k32jxbh which will automatically open a pdf file (Adobe Acrobat) of the Bibliography, or by using the QR Code embedded on the next page:

INDEX

ABOUT THE AUTHOR

Gabriella Kortsch, Ph.D. (Psychology) is also the author of the bestselling *Rewiring the Soul* (2011) and *The Tao of Spiritual Partnership* (2012). She works in private practice with an international clientele in southern Spain using an integral focus on body, mind and soul. Also an international speaker and radio broadcaster, she teaches workshops, posts on her blogs, and publishes a monthly newsletter in English and Spanish. She has three sons.

Contact details for Gabriella Kortsch, Ph.D. are as follows:

Websites: http://www.gabriellakortsch.com

http://www.advancedpersonaltherapy.com

Blogs: http://www.rewiringthesoul.com

http://www.taoofspiritualpartnership.com

http://www.powerofyourheart.com

Email: info@advancedpersonaltherapy.com

17640242R00151

Printed in Great Britain
by Amazon